THE CONTEMPORARY DISCUSSION SERIES

NAMING GOD

OTHER TITLES IN THE GOD SERIES

NAMING GOD

EDITED BY
ROBERT P. SCHARLEMANN

A NEW ERA BOOK

PARAGON HOUSE
New York

Published in the United States by
Paragon House Publishers
2 Hammarskjold Plaza
New York, NY 10017

A New Ecumenical Research
    Association Book

Library of Congress Cataloging in Publication Data
Main entry under title:

Naming God.

    (God, The Contemporary Discussion Series)
    "A New ERA book."
    Bibliography
    Includes index.
    1. God—Name—Addresses, essays, lectures.
2. God—Addresses, essays, lectures. 3. Trinity—
Addresses, essays, lectures. I. Scharlemann,
Robert P.   II. Series.
BL473.N36   1985   291.2'11'014   85-9327
ISBN: 0-913757-22-5 (hardbound)
ISBN: 0-913757-23-3 (softbound)

Contents

INTRODUCTION

ROBERT P. SCHARLEMANN

In Augustine's definition, theology is *sermo de Deo*—"talk about God." But who is the one named "God"? Is "God" another name for ultimate reality, or is "ultimate reality" another name for God? Which designation, in other words, serves the purpose of showing who or what the talk concerns and which is a second appellation for the same one? Such questions, not to mention the traditions of discussing the divine names, indicate that names have played a special role in the *sermo de Deo*. What that role is, is discussed from different perspectives, and with regard to different religious and theological traditions, in the essays collected for the present volume. The theoretical perspectives range from Caponigri's "icon" (in the broad sense of *eikon,* a real image) to Kasher's anti-idolist interpretation of religious language, and from the theist to the naturalist and nontheist; and the traditions are representative of all parts of the globe. No effort has been made to cover all possible topics; but we have tried to call attention to some of the basic questions and materials and to do so in such a fashion that the essays will be intelligible to readers with not more than a general basic knowledge of religious thought. The essays are, roughly, of two types—those whose primary interest is theoretical or methodical and those whose concern is primarily with the material content of one or more of the religious traditions. Since each of the contributors wrote his or her essay without having read the others, it will perhaps be of some assistance to the reader if this introduction provides a brief sketch of the connections among the essays and themes.

Part one contains three essays on theoretical foundations. In his opening essay, "Naming the Unnamable," Rayan discusses, with examples from many bodies of literature, the nature and purpose of names of the divine or the ultimate. The question of whether names are only conventional labels (so that, as the Shakespearean dictum has it, a rose by any other name would smell as sweet) or have a real connection to what they name has occupied philosophical discussion at least since the *Cratylus* and *Protagoras* of Plato. In those dialogues, Plato finds something to be said for both the conventional and natural theories without being able to decide clearly for the one or the other—though, in the voice of Socrates, he expresses his own inclination toward the natural theory. This discussion is enriched by investigations into other traditions, as Rayan's treatise illustrates.

If names are one means through which the named reality makes itself known, they do not yet settle the question of the kind of knowledge they mediate. The second essay undertakes to answer this question. Caponigri sets forth, in the context of a general epistemology, the nature of imagination and its function in making connection with the divine, the *theon*. From everyday experience, we are acquainted with the way in which our senses are the means through which objects can be presented to us for apprehension and cognition. Less familiar, or, at least, less clearly delineated in standard theories of knowledge, is the way in which imagination does the same thing, with absent objects. It is through imagination that we can have before our mind things that are not actually present to our senses—a scene that we remember, for example, or a possible event that we anticipate. But there is an important distinction, which Caponigri is interested in clarifying, between two kinds of images: the symbol and the icon. Symbols *re-present* absent things; icons, by contrast, *invoke* them. This distinction enables the author to come to terms with an objection sometimes voiced against symbols as vehicles of knowledge, namely, that symbols can present the realities they signify only in an anthropomorphic way, according to the features of the receiving person, and that symbols therefore do not present us with a real knowledge of the thing on its own. Caponigri argues that because an icon does not present or re-present that to which it refers but, instead, invokes it—that is, calls upon it to appear in its own features or traits—an iconic image is not subject to that objection.

Whereas Caponigri's essay deals with the issue of how imagination is related to knowledge, Jelly's has to do with the interplay between literal (analogical) and symbolic language in the knowledge of mystery. It was E. Przywara who, several decades ago,

called attention to the constitutive importance of the *analogia entis,*
"the analogy of being," in the philosophical, or "scientific," theology which was first worked out in the Middle Ages and which has
been a major strand in the Western monotheistic theologies. Jelly,
following Macquarrie's discussion and modifying it somewhat by
reference to Aquinas, presents a lucid treatise of what has become a
highly ramified and often very subtle discussion of symbol and
analogy.

The five essays of the second part of the book have to do with
names that are used in different religious traditions. Adewale and
Ansah work out the conception of deity, or of ultimate reality, as it
is contained in some of the African religions—among the Yoruba
and Ibo tribes in Nigeria (Adewale) and the Buem and Akan in
Ghana (Ansah). Both authors reach a similar conclusion from the
examination of the various names and attributes of deity. Contrary
to what one might at first think when one notices the similarity of
these conceptions of deity to the creator God of Christianity, the
African religions did not borrow the conception from Christian
missionaries; the evidence seems to indicate, rather, that it arose
within those religions even before the appearance of Christianity.
The investigations also disclose that speaking of God in the context
of everyday occurrences need not be, in all religions, the problematic matter that it has become in contemporary Christianity.

Eugen Rosenstock-Huessy once remarked that only those languages which have been nourished by Jewish and Christian Scriptures are able to make a distinction between God and the world.
Other thinkers, such as Dietrich Bonhoeffer, Rudolf Bultmann, and
Friedrich Gogarten, have remarked that there is—more cautiously
one might say that there seems to be—a connection between that
biblical linguistic tradition and the objectifying attitude toward
nature that is characteristic of modern science; for only a sharp
distinction between God and the world, as it is contained in the
biblical name of God as the creator, makes it possible to investigate
the causal connections among happenings in the world without
having to fear that doing so will invite punishment from invisible
demons. But one of the consequences of this objectifying attitude is
the loss of a living connection between human subjects and the
world of nature. Lee's essay points this out by drawing a clear
contrast between Chuang Tzu's view of nature and that of Christian supranaturalism on such matters as the personal character of
deity, the relation of religion and morality, the ultimate evaluation

of nature, and the way of salvation. The author concludes by suggesting a meeting of these opposed views in such theologies as those of Paul Tillich and John A. T. Robinson, in which transcendence is detached from "the projection of supranaturalism."

Nontheistic Buddhism, of the Śramaṇa tradition, might seem to present an even sharper contrast to monotheistic theologies. In his essay, Marasinghe argues for the historical point that this form of Buddhism did not arise out of opposition to Western theism or to the Upanishad philosophical tradition, but rather represents an intra-Buddhist development in which the older Śramaṇa tradition asserted its critique of the Brahmanic view of a supreme creator God, as found in the Pali Canon. The criticism rested upon there being no verification or experiential confirmation of the things asserted about this creator God. The Śramaṇic interest was to maintain the possibility of being able to find such confirmation through one's own experience, although the experience required is not everyday sense experience but that of the state of trance; and one of the concomitants of that interest is a conception of the divine and human in which the gods are not necessarily superior to the humans.

Concluding this part of the volume is an essay on one specific name: Nicholas of Cusa's formulation of the name of God as "the not other (li non aliud)." In twentieth-century theology, considerable attention has been paid to Anselm of Canterbury's formulation of the name of God as "that than which a greater cannot be thought (id quo majus cogitari nequit)." Karl Barth, for example, found a key in Anselm's wording for working out his own theology, and Charles Hartshorne saw in it the whole content of metaphysics. But the treatise by Nicholas, who is otherwise known for his conception of the infinite as involving a coincidentia oppositorum, a "coming together of opposites," has been left without consideration.

The first two essays in the third part, which raises some contemporary issues in the speaking of God, reflect some of the history of the genesis of the present volume. These essays were originally presented and discussed at a conference, sponsored by the New Ecumenical Research Association (New ERA), which was to have been held on the island of Trinidad but which in the last moment had to be moved to Ft. Lauderdale. The name of the island would naturally bring to mind the Christian name of God as triune. In his essay, Buri proposes an existentialist interpretation of the doctrine of the trinity, in which the imagery of Father, Son, and Spirit and the theological conceptualizations, which might of themselves suggest remnants of a mythological way of thinking that makes no sense today, are instead shown to be a true apprehension of personality; he argues, in fact, that the trinitarian doctrine is unintelligible just to the degree that we do not understand personality. Oduyoye, similarly, takes her starting point in the questionability of the traditional doctrine. She then sets forth a way in which the doctrine "makes sense" as a devotional model serving certain functions in human life. Its ethical function, for example, is to bring about a reassessment of where salvation lies; its sacramental function, to stand for participation rather than hierarchy in the organization of life.

In his essay, Grödal indicates some ways in which what we understand by the name "God" at all is conditioned by an ontology. This is true even of biblical writings. He undertakes, therefore, to delineate a biblical ontology which involves a network of three interrelated notions: the revelation of negative transcendence (indicated in the contrast in meaning between saying "X is not-Y" and saying "X is-not Y"), the polarity of God and man with a point of contact in verbal language, and the propositional nature of biblical language. Since the biblical is one among several possible ontologies, the essay concludes by proposing an answer to the question of a meta-ontological standpoint from which the different ontologies can be brought in touch with one another.

With the last essay, "Talk of God and Minimal Judaism," we return to a theoretical discussion, this time of the meaning of *sermo de Deo* in the context of Judaism. Kasher defines three elements that constitute "minimal Judaism" (that is, elements that are essential to all forms of Judaism, however diverse otherwise)—it is governed by constitutive rules, it is total, and it is radically opposed to idolatry. Kasher then explores the theory that talk of God, which comes into play when basically new problems arise that have to be resolved by going back to the normative roots of the society, is not assertive but is normative in purpose—it directs the follower to "observe an anti-idolist code of practice." Similarly, he proposes that the language of prayer is a "formal as-if context" (a kind of play), the point of which is to guard against any worship of the human by playing the role, in supplication, of "naturally weak human beings."

Part One:
THEORETICAL FOUNDATIONS

1

Naming the Unnamable

SAMUEL RAYAN

Names, Not Labels

In an introduction to a collection of prayers Swami Sambuddhānanda writes: "The names of Indra, Varuṇa, Agni, Soma, Āditya and other Gods which have been used in many places in the Vedas are but different appellations of the one Eternal Being. A mere superficial study of the Vedas may not reveal the unity underlying the multiplicity of these names; but whosoever reads between the lines of the Vedic texts cannot but understand them as different attributes or aspects of the same Supreme Being."[1]

The idea of unity in multiplicity and the mystery of names finds expression in the oldest of the world's Scriptures, the Vedas: "Truth (Reality) is one: Sages call it by various names," says the Rig Veda. The idea is part of a consistent pattern of thought, and no mere stray intuition. "The One Existent is conceived as many." And again, "The One Glory manifests itself in various ways."[2] The truth expressed here lies at the basis of Hinduism's open, tolerant, non-dogmatic, and assimilative character.

Are the divine names here being treated lightly, as labels which may be transferred, combined and piled up at will? Not likely. We must give full weight to the express subject of the first citation from the Rig Veda. If it is the Sages, persons dedicated to careful thought and serious search, that call the One by many names, we are face to face with a responsible act—a thought-out response to some compelling truth which they have encountered. Are the Sages doing what the Stoics did centuries later when they attempted to overcome polytheism by transferring all the names to one God, Zeus? Perhaps, provided the Stoics did not think of names as mere labels.

A name is rarely, if ever, a simple label. It is not wholly true that a rose would smell as sweet by any other name. The concrete experience of a rose would, I imagine, differ from that of a gulab. A name

3

not only denotes something, but also carries a wealth of connotations which it has acquired in the history of its usage and through which it invests the reality denoted with certain lights and shades of meaning, with certain tonalities and fragrances and suggestive power, or *dhvani*. These would not be the same if another name were substituted. Besides the riches of historical experience, a name embodies another, an originating experience as well. Every name arises out of an encounter between reality and people. It expresses a human group's response to reality's self-disclosure in a given place and time. No name, then, may be looked upon as purely arbitrary, external and subjective, even if it is not always possible to trace back to the original experience from which the name came to birth. The fact that at times people change names (as do san yasins, monks and nuns, popes, etc.) is no proof that names are exchangeable labels. Quite the contrary. This fact is proof indeed that names matter and have links with life and its meaning. "When people fight for their gods, they fight for their souls and their identity." They fight to defend the names of their gods and not for a label or "the copyright of a label." They fight for something substantial. True, the names of the God are the fruit of our naming. But "we name according to the self-disclosure of the 'named.'" Nominalism is a modern epidemic. God is not "a Kantian thing-in-itself to which then we stick our tags."[3]

Panikkar sums up "the dialectics of the name of God" in a series of what he calls "kairological moments." Before the rise of the great religions with their cultural and spiritual complexity, it was believed that "each God is a local God with a local name, his proper name," which stood revealed in myth. Meeting with different traditions or gaining of deeper insight into the mystery of God led to early realization that God has several names. But then a plurality of names was soon matched by a plurality of Gods, one God corresponding to each name. Then followed the discovery of a basic unity among the Gods: The many Gods are only different manifestations of a single and unique supreme power. No single name exhausts the divinity. No name is *the* name of God. There must therefore be a hidden name of God which is his true name, his adequate expression, and is known through revelation. One may have thought that the divine name is hidden and unknown because God has chosen to keep it so, and that he discloses it to his devotees. Soon there dawned the awareness that to be unknown is the essence of the secret name. "God has a name that is in itself intrinsically

4

hidden." The name of God is an interrogation. "God is a question that is always open, his name is the simple question about him, to find him is to seek him; to know him means not to know him." He is an interrogative pronoun: Who? Immediately a question arises about this question. Is not our question about God in its depths a question about us, about our destiny and the meaning of our life? Here Buddhism comes in to point out that neither question has a proper answer; that silence on the matter may be the path to the understanding of reality. But silence is no answer. It is itself a question. It silences all meaningless questions. One therefore no longer asks questions. One lives, one returns to daily life, but on a higher plane, where there is no attempt any more to discourse on God. But in the silence of the heart the Father is adored in spirit and in truth.[4]

Mystery of Names

Some such dialectic is found in all human attempts to name reality. Any given name names and fails to name. It reveals and leaves a great deal undisclosed, and we know it. It situates reality and points at the same time to the element of reality that escapes all attempts to grasp it and enclose it in a set of syllables. We keep adding new names. The more precious the reality, the greater the number of names we invent. Every name tends to break out of itself and transcend itself, and stretch into the future and the beyond. We are ever at the task of naming the unnamable. We suspect some affinity between divine and human names, divine and human realities.

Some names are descriptive. They underscore and convey certain aspects of reality, certain of its activities, functions and relationships. And as these are many, there can be many names and synonyms. It is the innate richness of reality that makes possible and calls for many names. A change of name or the introduction of a synonym alters the perspective on reality, affects its image in the mind, shifts the focus of our experience of it, modifies the emphasis, and opens up a new way of understanding it. Other names (of institutions, for instance, or of persons) are expressive of purposes or ideals, of projects and programs, of wishes and hopes. Names of persons (divine and human) are bound up with profound experiences of love, respect, admiration, and adoration which they carry and convey, which they evoke, renew, deepen, and confirm. What they evoke, imply, and suggest through their *vyanjana* or suggestive power is much more the loved and adored one's name than is the *lakṣaṇa* or the spoken, explicit appellation. Such names are meeting places of trust and intimacy. They are temples of doxology and celebration. They are not definitions or concepts, but living relationships.

This may explain in part the mystical importance given to names in most cultural traditions. To a Semite, for instance, "the name establishes a mystic union between the knower and the known. To know the name of another is in some sense to have him in one's soul. To pronounce his name is to make him present here."[5] The Old Testament seems to view names as expressions of the inmost being of reality, and especially of the essence of personality. To disclose one's personal name is to surrender the inmost citadel of one's self and hand over its keys. It is to lay oneself open to the reality, power, influence, needs, and love of the other. This view of names is fraught with consequences when God reveals his name to people and people name him and name themselves to him.

In India, to give a name to a boy is to bestow on him personality, distinction, and selfhood, and thus to free him from evil. The greater the number of names given, the greater the number of social relationships established and the fuller the liberation achieved from evil.[6] A potential energy resides in the name. It can be translated into effective power by using it, for instance, in an oath. The Jews were afraid of uttering the divine name Yahweh lest it should cause a dangerous discharge of divine power. To give a name is both to empower and to exert power.[7] The power of names can be used to bless and liberate people or to be maneuvered to suit selfish purposes and harm others. As the creator of the world, Yahweh names the stars and gives them their reality. He calls the people of Israel by name and takes possession of them in order to judge them and to protect them and through them to promote the cause of justice.[8] Symbolic destruction of someone's name insures the destruction of the bearer of the name. In the Soma sacrifice, one can burn up an enemy by consecrating oneself to Agni (fire) and mumbling the enemy's name. One can also protect oneself by entrusting one's name to some material object which is then kept safe beyond the reach of unfriendly forces.[9] It was a Gnostic belief that demons could be controlled through knowledge of their names.[10]

The mystery and power of the name throws light on the solemnity which attends a name-giving, *nāmakaraṇa,* ceremony, and the care shown in the choice of names. The occasion is rich in customs,

6

conventions, and rites as well as in mythology relating to it. Meaningful words and names of gods, heroes, ancestors, flowers, stars, precious stones, holy places, etc., are chosen as names in the hope that their bearers will share in the qualities and fortunes of the original. The Laws of Manu stipulate that the first part of a Brahmin's name should denote something auspicious and the second part imply happiness, while a Kṣatriya's name should point to power and protection, a Vaiśya's should promise industriousness and prosperity, and a Śudra's should reflect his menial status and service. Hiraṇyakeśin Gṛyha Sūetra adds a third name which should be kept secret, since it is a ritually generative force and is the part that survives death. As the name is the substance of the person, what survives is the name-person, the name-soul.[11] Change of names which indicate or accompany change of character, status, office or relationship is additional witness to the importance and mystery that we attach to names.[12]

Naming God

Name has creative power. According to Egyptian texts of the Heliopolitan priesthood (c. 2480–2137 B.C.), the "pre-existent Ultimate Source of all things was created by the utterance of his name, and so he became Khepri, he who exists by himself."[13] That means it named itself into existence with clear and reflexive awareness of itself as the ultimate source of all further possible names and realities. Name is reality, existence, distinctive consciousness, and power. We know that it is by being called and named that our identity, social self, and personhood come alive, grow, and develop. The Akkadian creation epic depicts the Fifty Great Gods as conferring on Marduk his fifty names, thus "assigning to him the powers of all the gods in the pantheon." It has been observed that the higher the standing of a God, the larger the number of his names. The *Viṣṇusahasranāma,* the thousand names of Vishnu (the great God whose redemptive *avatāras* fill a major part of his Hindu consciousness), would be an example, imitated by I. C. Chacko in his Christusahasranāma.[14]

The key to the nature of the Gods has been sought, by Hesiod for instance, in the etymology of their names. Many divine names derive from the reputed functions of the Gods. Epithets and adjectives describing their functions later become their personal names. Some names describe the terrible and the unapproachable aspects of the divine which, according to Plato, befit the gods, while others tell of beauty, affection, and tenderness. Thus Devī is Kālī as well as Mother. Rudra the terrible and Shiva the auspicious name the same God whose *nṛtya* ranges from the gracious *lāsya* to the earthshaking *tāṇḍava*. Each divine name is, as von Rad suggests, a "verbal cult practice." "Each authentic name is a real theophany."[15]

In the Old Testament, God's name is his revealed nature, his character as the savior of his people. His reality is at once transcendent and immanent, hidden, unfathomable, ontologically remote, but dynamically near. The gap is bridged by various manifestations such as the angel, the face, the glory, the name. Of these "the name" is the most comprehensive and the most significant, and is, in fact, often used, especially in post-exilic literature, as a synonym for God.[16] H. Bietenhard makes the point that one of the most fundamental and essential features of biblical revelation is the fact that God is not without a name by which he can, and is to be, invoked.[17] God is not thought of as nameless even when in the Jewish period his name is considered too holy, too dangerous to pronounce. Still on two occasions the (divine) name is withheld. The one that wrestles in the night with Jacob refuses to reveal his name in spite of being pressed to tell it. The man of God, the angel of Yahweh, who appears to Manoah and his wife, also declines to disclose his name. "Why ask my name? How can you ask my name? It is a mystery, a name of 'wonder.'"[18] God is not nameless, but his name is mysterious, wonderful, unspeakable. He is heard and touched in the dark of the night that envelops him, in which we sense his nearness and his distance, and experience our strength and our weakness. His name is revealed in the wonders that he does rather than in sounds and syllables borrowed from our speech. Jacob is to learn the name of the one that wrestled with him in the divinely wrought events and experiences of subsequent years. Manoah and his wife will come to know the name in the wonder of the birth and life of Samson. The revealed God is the hidden God; his name is made known more in his deeds than in our words. He names himself in his works and discloses his self in saving interventions. His name has its roots in his heart, for his name is love. But it branches out and realizes itself in our history. In our history God's name becomes summons, missions, struggle for liberation.

Yahweh is God's historical name in the Old Testament. It is central to biblical tradition and is of primary significance. Yahweh defines the nature of deity as deeply involved in the experience, struggle, and destiny of oppressed people. It is a powerful expression of God's historical dealings with situations of indignity and injustice, and of his personal rule and action on behalf of freedom and the rights of the despised and the abused. According to the Elohist sources of the Pentateuch, Yahweh is the exclusive covenant name made known in the context of God's oppressed people's united struggle for liberation and their agreed Ten Word program for a new style of human group-life based on justice, freedom, and fellowship within the mercy of the original liberating action. The Priestly sources present the name as the climactic point of a history of name-revelations. Until the time of Abraham, God is known as Elohim. The patriarchs knew him as El Shaddai. In the days of Moses and the Exodus struggle a new name, Yahweh, is made manifest. Not that it was arbitrarily withheld, but that only now was there this historical action for liberation out of which the name could emerge and from which it could draw substance and meaning.[19] The revelation of the name is made, like all revelation, in history and as history. History is our access to the inaccessible, and its to us. God names himself and is invoked by us in terms of actual situations and experiences. In a cosmic culture God is El Shaddai, and the imagery seems to come from nature, the mountains, their sublimity, stability, and strength. But with the organizing of action and struggle for justice and liberty, God is Yahweh and the imagery is from the movement of history and looks to the future.

Several lines of interpretation of the tetragram YHWH have been attempted. The reply of God is an evasion, said Loisy. Others have said that it is an affirmation of himself as the self-existing one; that it means that he is the only one having real existence; that he is the one who is; that he is one who causes all things to be; or (relating the name to Arabic, hawa = to devote oneself to), that it points to one who demands exclusive devotion, or better, to one who is passionately devoted to Israel; and finally that the name means one who will be what he will be and intends to be.[20] Jose Miranda, with support from Michael Allard, Martin Noth, Paul Joüon, and Horst D. Preuss, expands the last line of thought mentioned above, and stresses the essential futureness denoted by the name. He links it up with God's action to form a people in justice and freedom "as the seed of future humanity in which, and only in which, he finally will be able to be."[21] God exists, reveals himself, possesses a name and discloses it: he does all this in his history-making action for justice, freedom, and fellowship; and it is in our corresponding collaborative action on behalf of a new earth where he can be god and we can be human that we can meet, hear, and invoke Yahweh. Yahweh is God's name becoming; Yahweh is God becoming.

The definitive disclosure of this mystery of God walking our earth, and coming to us and to himself, and making a name for himself in making with us a history of justice and compassion is had in Jesus Christ. Jesus, in his life of service to the people, in his struggle unto death for the downtrodden, and in his subversion of the forces of alienation and despair, is himself the eschatological name of God. The name above all names which God gave to Jesus was itself built through a history of self-emptying which was not only metaphysical but sociohistorical. It was built through a history of learning obedience through suffering, of opting for the outcasts of society and braving death for their liberation. With him, therefore, God shared his own names and power, enabling him to reveal these as promise and hope for all who are powerless and oppressed. The Father's name which Jesus then makes known is not just the term *Abba*. It is rather the whole involvement of God in the world, his passionate participation in the processes of history, his compassion for the neglected people, the tears he sheds, the cry of his heart, the wounds of humanity which he bears, his immersion in the Jordan of their suffering and struggle and the hope that is growing within them.

The It, the I, the Saccidananda

We return now to the Indian scene. Here we have to pay attention not only to names but also, and especially, to pro-names. Is the Deity He or She or It? All three, and beyond. The reference here is not to divine pairs like Vishnu and Lakṣmī, Shiva and Pārvati, or Rādhā and Krishna, but to the absolute and to its mystery, of which the pairs are revelatory symbols and revealing names. The absolute is Puruṣa, Śakti, Brahman, Father and Mother of the world and the ground and home of all that is. The eternal is Ardhanāriśvara as well as the self of every self. Actually the self cannot be half something and half something else. The self is completely Nāri and wholly Iśvara. The *ardha* is the symbol for unity and oneness. Nor are the pairs to be so understood that the masculine should represent the changeless absolute, and the feminine the changing phenomenal. What is revealed as differentiation, complementarity, and unity is the undifferentiated riches of the depths of the eternal, which we must represent both as Rādhā and Krishna and as surpassing them in a transcendence within which they are present and are one.[22]

At that level perhaps the divine name is *om*. Om encompasses Brahman which enfolds and pervades the universe.

This syllable Oṁ is the whole universe . . .
What was and is and yet to be,—
All of it is Oṁ;
And what ever else the three times transcends—
That too is Oṁ.[23]

Oṁ is composed of the waking state, the dreaming state, the state of deep sleep without dreams, and what is beyond: the mass of wisdom made of bliss. Oṁ is made up of three letters, "A," "U," and "M," and of a fourth which is beyond letters; it has no components; it is devoid of duality. In om the world is resolved and developments come to rest; it is auspicious. Such is om, the very self.[24] Oṁ is indeed holy and supreme; it is the sound form of the self. Feminine, masculine, neuter—these are its sex-forms; fire, wind, sun—these are its light-forms; earth, atmosphere, sky—these are its word-forms; etc. This syllable om is the higher and the lower Brahman.[25] But beyond om or in the heart of it, at its highest or deepest summit is silence, and that is the ultimate name of the divine.[26]

Further still, if the absolute is the real self, if it is ever the subject and never an object, then the self's name is always "I," while creatures are the "he," the "she," and the "it." These can be addressed by "I" and enabled to enter upon a process of becoming "thou," a participant in a dialogue and a face-to-faceness in which breaths meet and mingle. Then we know its deep, intimate name by becoming it.

We can recall here but a few of the numberless names, epithets, metaphors, images, symbols and descriptions of the supreme self enshrined in the devotional, spiritual, artistic and theological works of India. One of the most fascinating symbols of the absolute is *Saccidānanda,* a cumulative name with a dynamic movement which takes you from reality (*sad*) to reality's own conscious, shining depth (*cit*) and thence, continuing the inward journey, to the profoundest center and source of reality itself which is bliss (ānanda), pure and infinite, the ultimate truth of being.[27]

The expression "Saccidānanda" seems to have arisen spontaneously from the heart of India's seers, when they tried to find some way of referring to the mystery which they intuited beyond the range of thought. The welcome given to this term in the tradition undoubtedly proves its affinity to the Hindu soul . . . for many hundreds of years it had been accepted in the spiritual vocabulary of India as one of the best symbols for the innermost mystery of God himself, so far at least as man is capable of stammering about it.[28]

In the Upanishads this person, this self, this immortality, this freedom from fear, this Brahman is also called "convergence of the beautiful," "bringer of the beautiful" and "bringer of light."[29] It is the great abode and support or home. Hidden and moving in the secret place (of the heart) is its name. It has been revealed. On it are centered and fixed all that move, breathe, and blink. Know that as being, and as nonbeing, as the one reality to be supremely desired, as the highest beyond the reach of man's understanding. He is the *parat-parah Puruṣaḥ* the person beyond the beyond to whom the man who knows and is thereby released from name and form may draw near as a river flows and finds its home in the ocean, leaving name and form behind.[30]

He is the Self of all,
all things experiencing, (enjoyer of all)
the Lord of all
more inward than what is most inward in all things.
(*sarvasyāntarāntarah*)
He is the Self without self. He indwells all.
He indeed is the Self within the heart.[31]

Nāma-Sādhana

In all the major Indian traditions we meet with the idea that the changeless eternal transforms itself into this evolving universe without losing fullness or transcendence—the nameless and the formless taken on names and forms. "Because he came to be, he [himself became] a contingent being, entered into contingent beings, and moves [among them]. He became the king of [all] contingent beings. Hence he is the Self both within and without."[32] This idea of the unnamable becoming a named part of creation is taken up and continued in Purāṇic prayers such as the following:

"May that supreme Lord who, devoid of name, form or end, yet took, for blessing those who adored his feet, names and forms through incarnations and exploits, be gracious to me."[33]

"The sin that has accrued to me . . . may all that sin disappear as a result of the recital of the Lord's names, Nārāyaṇa, Govinda, Hari, and Kṛṣṇa, even as a cup of salt in water."[34]

According to the Purāṇas the utterance of the Lord's name destroys sin completely, even when the utterance is unintended, or is done in jest, or involuntarily, or in derision.[35] This is an obvious hyperbole, since the authors of the Purāṇas critize as aberrations the empty forms and rites which parade as devotion in place of the realization of the Lord's universal presence. The overstatement is meant to call attention to the beauty and effectiveness of devotion to the Lord's name.

"The Lord's names are medicines; they are sacred mantras; they are the way to salvation in the other world, they are all the other good things, too; through them all acute miseries are destroyed; meditate only on those names of the Lord." So writes the Śaivite Jnānasambandha in the seventh century A.D. A thousand years later we find the devotion to the name as alive as ever. Around 1700 we find Stridhara Venkaṭeśa working in southern India to promote the recital of the Lord's name and the practice of *bhajans* or congregational singing. From him we have a "Hymn of Sixty Verses" (*ākhyā-ṣaṣṭi*) on the Lord's name. Here are a few lines from it: "O Name of the Lord! Let there be the Vedas by hundreds, and by hundreds the piles of Purāṇas and Āgamas; are these capable of giving the thought of the Lord without you? On the other hand, you who remove all weariness completely without any effort, can bestow that thought of the Lord without the aid of any of these."[36]

This tradition of Nām Bhajan and Nāma Sādhana received a new impetus in the nineteenth century which has reached into the twentieth century through such saints as Swami Mahārāji Sibdayal Singh (1818–1878), Thakkur Bhaktivinode (b. 1838), Vijayakṛṣṇa Goswāmin (1841–1899), Prabhu Jagadbandhu (1871–1921) and Mother Anandamayi (b. 1896).

Swami Maharaj proposes not a new religion but a new way in which Sabda Yoga and Nāma Japa combine. The true name of God gives us salvation. No liberation is possible without practice of the name. The name reaches us and is experienced at two levels, and has two forms: the *Varṇātmaka* and the *Dhvanyātmaka*. The Varṇātmaka is the name we spell out in thought or speech or ink. There can be many such names, but none of them is the real name; they are symbols, signs, or sacraments of the real one. Their repetition helps concentrate attention and make spiritual progress toward the point and the moment of perception of the Dhvanyātmaka Nama in the depths of one's heart. Dhvanyātmaka Nama is the one eternal sound and word, the divine melody continuously emanating from the Lord and resounding, the same, in every heart, and drawing and enabling every soul to hear it, to become attuned to it, to become it, and merge into the celestial music and be released into the transcendent divine harmony. This name is a limitless, unrepeatable, unutterable utterance. Swami Maharaj called this the Rādhāswāmi Path, where Radha is the "soul" and Swami is the "Lord."[37]

The Rādhāswāmi Path belongs with the great tradition of Vac, Sabda and Dhvani, of Pūrva Mīmāmṣā and Nyāya, of Bhartṛhari and Anandavardhana.[38] It is allied also with the path of Sabda practice or Nādānusamdhāna, described at length in works on Hatha Yoga. Nāda is deeply vibrating sound. As such it helps concentration and leads to *Samādhi,* "ecstasy." But the chanting of the divine name accompanied by breath-control goes even deeper; it is great aid to the development of *Bhakti,* "devotion."[39] Rādhāswāmi reminds one in particular of Thyāgarāja (1767–1847), the great southern Indian composer, whose songs are noteworthy not only for their fervent devotion and their ethical and spiritual quality, but also "for proclaiming the role of music as an easier spiritual path than even Yogi practices." But music can be *sādhana,* "spiritual exercise," only if it is cultivated with devotion to the Lord. Thyāgarāja writes:

O Mind! devotion associated with the ambrosia of the notes and melodies of music is verily paradise and salvation . . .

To know and realize the nature of sound . . . is itself bliss . . . Likewise the knowledge of the various resonant centers of the body from which emanate the seven glorious notes of music.

Through philosophical knowledge one attains salvation only gradually after several births; but he who has knowledge of melodies along with natural devotion to God becomes a liberated soul here and now.[40]

The core of Nāma Sādhana is *Nāma Japa,* which is very similar to the Jesus Prayer familiar to Orthodox Christian tradition.[41] The road to perfect faith is complete dedication to the constant recitation of the divine name which in its essence is identical with God, and is indistinguishable from Rama or Krishna. The divine name is not an audible sound expressed through letters, but a spark of the divine light "carrying in it the illimitable omnipotence of God."[42] The name, when imparted by a qualified master, possesses great potency and "carries a spiritual energy concentrated in a word which serves as the medium of expression." Ānandamayi, however, denies the need of dependence on a *guru,* or of hard yoga practices. The power of the name is independent of any *dikṣa* or "ascetic self-discipline."[43] Bhaktivinode would agree with Ānandamayi and insist that Nam Bhajan is not bound by any rule.[44]

The immediate effect of uninterrupted practice of *Nāma Japa* may be a sense of spiritual upheaval, an intense burning sensation in the body, a feeling that the name is circulating along all the intra-organic channels of the physical frame, or an appearance of the name or of its symbols on the palm or back of the hands. But the ultimate fruit of uninterrupted practice is the appearance of the name in person before the spiritual eye of the devotee; the manifestation of the proper form of the name (swarūpa), which is identical with the spiritual form of Krishna; and further, the generation of Bhakti and the transformation of the *Sādhaka* or exercitant into the glory of the name itself; and finally, the fountaining forth of ineffable joy in the purified and liberated self.[45]

Apophatism and Convergence of Silences

This impressive spiritual witness deserves respect and may not be ignored. It is within such human experience that questions about God will have to be placed and investigated. One such scrutiny, quite a searching one, comes from the Buddha, who points out that on the admission of believers themselves, God is transcendent, unknowable, unnamable, unlike anything we can see, touch, imagine, or think. If a transcendent exists, it surpasses our being and our thought and all our attempts to name it. To name it would be to situate it among namable beings, to enclose it in our categories, and so to kill it. God cannot be named. Indeed, there is no need to name God for he has no name because there is nothing that has this name. The Buddha refused to name him. "For the Buddha, eliminating the name of God is the supreme religious undertaking."[46] Panikkar concludes that the problem of God does not lie in the realm of theory. "It does not belong to the realm of the word, but to the kingdom of silence."[47]

Buddhist apophasis is radical. But a profound apophatic consciousness is present in the language of believers and mystics themselves. In nearly all mystic thought God is admittedly nameless and ineffable. The Upanishads insist that Brahman resembles nothing in our experience, that every representation and affirmation about God has to be denied at once with emphatic, repeated *na iti, na iti,* "That Self is not this, not this, It is incomprehensible." "Not this, not this, for there is nothing higher than this, he is not this"; or, "No, No! for there is nothing higher than this No." "That Self is not this, not this. It is incomprehensible, for It is never comprehended."[48] Mystics are uncompromisingly apophatic. They ask: "By what should one know that by which all this is known? By what should know the Knower?"

That incomprehensible one, O Gargi,
is the Seer who is never to be seen, the Hearer who is never to be heard,
the Knower who is never to be known.[49]

Brahman is the knower, the subject. He can never become the object of our knowing or naming activity. Also, in the Rādhāswāmi tradition the Dhanyatmak name is inexpressible. Its secret nobody knows, and the Lord is unknowable and inexpressible.[50]

In the *Bhagavad Gita* Krishna declares his many names, describing himself as the beginning of the gods, the source of all, the all-highest Brahman, the self in the heart of all, time imperishable and all-devouring death. But finally and most significantly, the list culminates in wisdom and silence. "The very silence of hidden, secret things am I/And the wisdom of the wise."[51] Maitri Upanishad makes the point explicit. There are two Brahmans: Brahman as sound (*śabda brahman*) and the soundless Brahman beyond. Those who know the Sound-Brahman get to the higher Brahman. The Brahman as sound is the syllable om. Its summit is silence, soundless, free from fear and sorrow.[52] It is not only silent but beyond our reach. We may think and speak and hear of him as a marvel, but "even after hearing no one whatsoever has known him."[53]

Even among Jewish mystics and thinkers apophatism is not absent, despite the Bible's clear position that God has a personal name. To Philo, God has no qualities, no personal name; his being can neither be conceived nor uttered. He is the nameless existing. "There is absolutely no name which fits my nature" says God in Philo's *Life of Moses.*[54]

Christian apophatism is far stronger and more persistent. The many names of God can be "transmuted into namelessness in that no name does justice to the Godhead." God is incomprehensible and therefore unknowable. The approach to him *via eminentiae* means that every affirmation has to be denied and transcended so that all along we remain with a negative theology, akin to the *neti neti* theology of the Upanishads. To eliminate all anthropomorphism, Clement of Alexandria would stick to a negative conception of God. "Nor can we say that God has shape or name." Names such as the One, the Father, God, etc., are strictly not appropriate. We employ them because we are incapable of finding true names and our minds need something to rest on.[55] Gregory Nazianzen is in agreement with this line of thought as the following lines from his *Hymn to God* testify:

You who are beyond, beyond all—
what other name befits you? . . .
Alone you are ineffable—
of every voice you are the source.
Alone you are unknowable—
from you all thought is born. . . .
Of all beings you are the End;
you are One, you are All, you are None; . . .
Bearer of all names, how shall I name you—
You alone the Unnameable? . . .
You are beyond, beyond all—
No other name befits you![56]

To Gregory of Nyssa every concept relative to God is a false likeness, an idol. There is only one name by which the divine nature can be expressed: "the wonder which seizes the soul when it thinks of God."[57]

Eastern Christianity in its theology, liturgy, and spirituality is marked by the apophatic which is a mystical approach as against the cataphatic, rational approach of the West since the Middle Ages. Both approaches are possible and valid, and must be held in dialectical relationship to each other. The apophatic holds that since God can never be the object of conceptual knowledge, all positive assertions about God are inadequate, "and, if taken literally, are simply untrue." It proceeds by unknowing. "It involves the conscious overcoming of concepts and propositions. Its conditions are faith, prayer, sacramental life, liturgical experience and ascetic purification."[58]

The way of unknowing is not unknown to the West. It was Augustine who said that God remains unknown in our knowledge and is known in our unknowing.[59] Aquinas admitted that we rather know what God is not, than what/who he is. *The Cloud of Unknowing* comes to us from some English country parson of the late fourteenth century. Since the Middle Ages, then, Western theology has always admitted, though without accent, that conceptual representation cannot reach God but can only indicate the direction in which God's attributes lie.[60]

But if that is the position of believers, why are they not Buddhists? If God is unknowable and unreachable, how could one say anything about him? On what grounds does one say that God exists, or is unknowable, or is beyond names, or that he does not exist?

Who Can Name Him?

The reply of believers is that the unknowability of God is not a conclusion deduced from reason and philosophy, nor a science gathered inductively from experiment and observation. God's inscrutability is not a matter of logic but of revelation and faith. It is an affirmation of faith-experience. God reveals himself and names himself. It is in his self-disclosure and self-communication into the depths of our personal being that we come to experience his own depths. We experience him as reality on which all the reality we are and know rests, and to which it points. In our faith-response to his revelation and self-gift, we touch him as the real of the real and know him as the unknowable. And we name him in the wake of his naming himself to us first. He names himself to us in loving and naming us into existence, and in continuing to come to us in a ceaseless dialogue of life and love. In faith we receive his names as sacraments pointing to, and conveying us into, his unspeakable name. For, "this Self cannot be attained by instruction, nor by intellectual (or sacrificial) power, nor even through much learning. He is to be attained only by the one whom the (self) chooses. To such a one the self reveals his own nature."[61] The Gita has the same teaching; it is the tradition of all religions. "Neither by the Vedas (nor by) sacrifices nor by study nor by gifts nor by ceremonial rites nor by severe austerities can I with his form be seen in the world of men by any one . . ."[62] To this election and revelation corresponds the faith which confesses the mystery and unknowability of the Lord.

But by worship of love addressed to me alone
Can I be known and seen
In such a form and as I really am . . .[63]

We are then dealing with two different kinds of knowledge, two
distinct levels of awareness. One is conceptual, the other is beyond
and deeper. One is reason, the other is spirit. One works with the
head, the other experiences with the heart. One may take pride in
science conquered and seized, the other can only rejoice in relationships freely given and freely received day by day. *The Cloud of
Unknowing* puts it briefly:

But only to our intellect is he incomprehensible;
not to our love . . .
Why, love may reach up to God himself even in this life—
but not knowledge.[64]

His love takes the initiative and our answering love comprehends
him as the incomprehensible, and knows him as the unknowable.
And so doing love is glad, and love has its own reason of which
reason knows nothing.

Brahman, therefore, is "known by an awakening" and is then
"seized upon by thought."[65] Accordingly, the Upanishadic tradition
has this description of him: "this is as it were like the lightning
which flashes forth or the winking of the eye." "Ah!—people say
when the lightning flashes, Ah! as they blink their eyes."[66] The
absolute is known and unknown, named and unnamed in the
Āśscarya, "the wonder," which strikes us, fills us, takes hold of us
and illumines and transports us, not as we "think" of God, as
Lossky says, but as Brahman self flashes on us suddenly, unexpect-
edly, undeservedly, surprising us, in the winking of an eye. Founda-
tionally the knowledge and the name are gifts.

There can be sudden shafts of light piercing the cloud of unknowing and giving us glimpses of the beyond. Out of this experience we may weave names for him which then we unweave
because they are never adequate. But there can also be a gradual,
unobtrusive growing of light upon our consciousness, like the quiet
coming of the dawn. We read in the Kena Upanishad, in the section
immediately preceding the lightning passage, the story of the beautiful lady, Umā Haimavatī, appearing in the sky and revealing the
identity of Brahman to three old gods who had been trying for
some time but in vain to discover who indeed that unfamiliar spirit
was who had made himself visible to them.[67] This is a case of a

progressive recognition of revelation in the medium of the beautiful in creation. The beautiful know him because they come from him and retain the memory and fragrance of his creative touch and breath; and because he himself is the "Convergence of the Beautiful."[68] Chiming in with this is the other story, in the Chāndogya Upanishad, of Satyakāma, whose instruction was delayed by his Guru. Creation, however, revealed to him the nature and the name of Brahman. At the bidding of his Guru he lived long years as a cow-herd, and therefore close to nature. The bull and the fire, a swan and a diver-bird disclosed to him the four quarters of Brahman, namely, the shining (*prakāśavān*), the endless (*anantavān*), the effulgent (*jyotiṣmān*) and the homely or the support-possessing (*āyatanavān*). On the boy's return to the house, the teacher found him radiant like a knower of Brahman. At the boy's request he taught him what nature had already communicated to him. With the human teacher, knowledge acquires a new, personal dimension, and becomes an interpersonal relationship and a social reality.[69]

There are many ways of communion between him and us—revelation in the heart, revelation in nature; sudden intuitions, imperceptibly growing consciousness; clear as lightning, obscure as clouds—but it is sure and sustained intercourse in sound and in silence, naming, not naming, searching ever for finer, richer, tenderer names. He names himself in naming us and enables us day by day to name him in naming us and our world.

Aum

This syllable oṁ is this whole universe . . .
What was and is and is yet to be,—
All of it is Oṁ;
And whatever else the three times transcends,—
That too is Oṁ.
For all this world is Brahman. This Self is Brahman.[70]

Nature, the human heart, and the heart of history are the place of Brahman's self-revelation and self-naming. They are organically connected and dialectically interactive like the points in a magnetic field or the parts of a living body. The possibilities of this truth are taken seriously and utilized as much by the Bhagavad Gita as by the Upanishads. In chapters 7 to 10 inclusive of the Gita, Krishna names himself in a variety of ways, some suggestive, some startling, but all in terms of natural objects and human activities both sacred and secular.

Of the whole universe the origin and dissolution am I.
I am the thread on which this universe is strung like pearls.
I am the flavor in water and fragrance in the earth.
And I am the light in sun and moon, and sound in space.
Father and mother of the world, teacher, friend and lover of all.
Of weapons I am the thunderbolt, of serpents Vāsuki,
and I am the dicing of tricksters.
Death am I, and Deathlessness, and Life in beings,
Source and seed, and the Self in the heart
and Time, and of hidden secret things the Silence.

But this revelation is made in the battlefield, in the arena of history. It is made to persuade Arjuna out of a false noninvolvement and inaction into struggle for the holding together and welfare of the world and the happiness of all living things. It is to equip the man for fight against insolent and aggressive power. The more Arjuna rids himself of paralysis and perplexity and commits himself to the Lord within the commitment to the task in hand, the more that profounder and more intimate revelations of the divine come to him. Keeping the structure and dynamics of the Gita in mind one could say that the revelation happens right within the struggle and deepens with action to win back and uphold the dignity and rights of the oppressed. It is by naming the people that the Lord is named.

What Krishna does is exactly what the Buddha does too, though with a plus. The plus is the openness to the beyond, the manifestation of Krishna's cosmic form in the very heart of the historical struggle. While Krishna admits limitless questions and is ready to travel the starry expanses of speculation, Buddha thinks it fallacious and idle to seek to pierce intellectually the mystery of existence. What is common to both is the accent on the here and the now. Buddha insists on a realistic sense of life as it is given, and refuses to replace reality with ideas. He makes us aware of our limits, centers us on the human task we can fulfill, and refuses to distract us from concrete commitments. He removes our preoccupation with orthodoxy in order to return us to the orthopraxis of the eight-fold path which leads to liberation. No longing for death, no pining after life, no desire to transgress reality, no questions about ultimates, no rebellion, no despair, no discouragement, no resignation, but simple acceptance of the human condition and straightforward commitment to better it.[71]

The Buddha may not have said it, but silence like his may lead us to the threshold where divinity may, or may not, be found. And compassion like his may be the best preparation to encounter God if there is one. If there is God, he will come to meet us, for we do not know him nor do we know the way to him.[72] But if he is there, he knows us and the way to us. He will want to be where broken people are being rebuilt, and where the outcasts are gathered in with reverence.

At this point the voice of the Buddha merges with the voice of Jesus, both calling for mercy and not for sacrifice, centering us on people and not on the "sabbath," demanding that we love one another, which means concrete responsibility for the hungry, the despised, the abused, and those left broken on the wayside. Jesus told the story of the good Samaritan. The Buddha told the story of the man pierced by an arrow. Both demand that we face facts and respond to the call of reality, and not escape into speculation. Both the Buddha and Jesus are agreed that no revelation and no religion, no god and no spirituality can justify the neglect and manipulation of people. But there is a plus in the position Jesus takes. He remains and would have us remain positively open to the irruption of reality from beyond the familiar horizons of our thought and experience, open to surprises, open to endless possibilities which are implied in the transcendence of the smallest compassion and in the tiniest effort, to better the human condition here and now. That openness is where the face of God begins to show and grow in clarity. That sense of transcendence is where the name of God begins to shape up and surpass itself.[73]

A tiny flower blooming in the field and fading in a day is, for Jesus, something that involves the whole of God and shows the wonder and the power of his creative love. The flower is a name of God. So is the bird in the sky, the rain that soaks the earth, the hills and the seas, and every living thing. The whole cosmos is a single icon and the one great, beautiful, picturesque name of God spoken and revealed. "I am the vine, I am the light, I am the bread and the way, I am the bright morning star," this lamb this lion.[74] Not only is the divine name being written on the forehead of the cosmos, but the evolving cosmos is the writing of the name.

The history people make and the culture they fashion with their toil, love, and struggles form a dynamic icon of God, and are the divine name unfolding. God is spelling it out with us and we with him. In the process, history itself gets its true name. For the two

names are inseparable: the one is in the other. Every person participates in this profound character and meaning of history. Every
person, made in God's image and called to become it, is a precious
word with which God is naming himself. When we grasp and take
hold of ourselves, we are naming ourselves, touching God and
sensing his own name. Strictly speaking we cannot name God, and
there is no need to. What we need to do, and it is beautiful, is to
become an invocation directed to God in response to his ceaseless
self-naming of us into ever richer existence. What we should be
glad to do is to care for his manifest name and image on earth. The
revelation is that the brother and the sister in need are the visibility
of his hidden name; often dispossessed and trodden underfoot, the
poor are his forgotten name. They are his intimate reality. To touch
them is to touch him, touch the pupil of his eye. To profane people
is to profane God's name. In honoring the poor, the name of God is
honored. The prayer that his name be held holy and experienced as
meaningful is (to be) directly followed by concern for rice for the
deprived, and forgiveness for the guilty who do the depriving. Rice
is a symbol for all the rights of the wretched of the earth. Within
their struggles God is present, making a name for himself.

His name is om. Om is nature and history, the history of freedom, the history of struggles for freedom and dignity, the history of
the oppressed, even the history of the oppressed Son of Man. His
name is God's name. His name is om, Amen.

To Sum Up

God alone knows who God is. He alone knows his name. He names
himself. But he names himself to us and names us to ourselves. We
are part of his self-naming activity; we are interior to his name. This
now is an ongoing process in an evolving cosmos and an unfolding
history. We may listen and respond to the name he is speaking. We
may contemplate his creation, help develop its potentialities, set
right our distortions of it, make and keep it beautiful, and let it serve
all God's people. We may respond by liberating history, building it
up in freedom, and rendering its desires, perceptions, and structures
truly human. Alienation of the earth and oppression of the unarmed
obstructs the emergence of God's name, wipes it off the face of the
earth, and creates atheism. The prophets perceived long ago the
connection between injustice and godlessness. Micah says of the
ruling classes: "When they have devoured the flesh of my people

and torn off their skins and crushed their bones . . . then they will cry out to Yahweh. But he will not answer them, he will hide his face . . ."[75] On the other hand, historical struggles for justice, freedom, and human authenticity, and efforts to build a human community in equality and peace, are divinely enabled human contributions to the naming of the name.

As history overcomes its alienation, as the oppressed liberate themselves and establish justice, as humankind grows into a fellowship of equality and freedom, the name will become clearer and holier. It will come to meet us, and enable us to become it beyond all ambiguity. To know God is to do justice.[76] Justice is his name. It is so hope-giving to see so many young, beautiful and strong people all over the world struggling to have this name written on the forehead and the heart of history.

To know God we must surrender to reality as well as wrestle with it. Historical reality, being in process, is ambiguous, and God's name comes to us within this ambiguity. We have to wrestle with reality as the Buddha did, and with God as did Jacob and Job and Jesus. Only then can we qualify to ask: What is your name? Without coming to grips with mystery (Jacob's antagonist comes in the night and hurries off as day breaks!), we cannot pass (as Job did pass) beyond hearsay,[77] and arrive at the point of face to face encounter. Without the wrestling we cannot ask from the midst of the anguish of our cross: God, our God, why have you forsaken us, why? It is through such nights and descending darkness, such agony and social crucifixion, such historical struggles of and with God that we can meet the name as it emerges from the depths of our hearts, the depths of human history and the depths of God, and comes to meet us.

NOTES

1. Swami Sambuddhānanda, *Vedic Prayers* (Bombay: Saxon Press, 1938, 1971), xi.

2. *Rig-Veda* 1.164, 46: ekam sadviprā bahudhā vadanti; 10.114, 5: ekam santam bahudhā kalpayanti, trans. H. H. Wilson, 1850 (Delhi: Cosmo Publications, 1977); *Atharva Veda* 13.3, 17: ekam jyotir bahudhā vibhāti, trans. W. D. Whitney (Cambridge: Harvard Oriental Series, 1908), vol. 8.

3. R. Panikkar, "Indian Theology: A Theological Mutation" (unpublished paper read in a seminar held in Pune, India, 1970).

4. R. Panikkar, *Myth, Faith and Hermeneutics: Cross-Cultural Studies* (New York: Paulist Press, 1979), 266–68, hereafter referred to as *MFH*.

5. D. J. Bourke, s. v. "God, Names of," in P. K. Meagher, T. C. O'Brien, and C. M. Ahern, eds., *The Encyclopedic Dictionary of Religion* (Washington, D.C.: Corpus, 1979), hereafter referred to as *EDR*.

6. P. V. Kane, *History of Dharmaśāstra* (Pune: Bhandarkar Oriental Institute, 1936), vol. 1, pt. 1, 238–54; Cf. *Śatapatha Brāhmaṇa* 6.1.3, 9.

7. Gen. 2, 2 Sam. 12:28, Ps. 49:11.

8. Ps. 147:4, Deut. 28:10, Isa. 42:1, 43:1, 63:19.

9. *Atharva Veda* 6.83, 2; *Kauṣitaki Brāhmaṇa* 7.3; J. Hastings, *Encyclopedia of Religion and Ethics* (Edinburgh: Clark, 1917), s. v. "Name," hereafter referred to as *ERE*.

10. Allegro, *The Sacred Mushrooms and the Cross* (Garden City, NY: Doubleday, 1970), 161; Cf. Mark 5:9, Jesus asking the unclean spirit to reveal its name.

11. Margaret and James Stutley, *A Dictionary of Hinduism: Its Mythology, Folklore and Development* (London: Harper & Row, 1977), s. v. "Name," hereafter referred to as *DH; Manusmṛti* 2.31–32, trans. G. Bühler, part of *The Sacred Books of the East,* ed. Max Müller (Oxford, 1886).

12. Gen. 17:5, 32:28, Isa. 62:2, Matt. 16:18.

13. Stutley, *DH,* s. v. "Name."

14. Ibid., with reference to E. O. James, *Tree of Life,* 138.

15. Gerhard von Rad, *Old Testament Theology* (London: Oliver and Boyd, 1962), 1:183f. Also Panikkar, "Indian Theology."

16. R. Abba, s. v. "Name," in G. A. Buttrick, ed., *Interpreter's Dictionary of the Bible* (New York: Abingdon Press, 1962), vol. 3, hereafter referred to as *IDB*.

17. H. Bietenhard, s. v. "Name," in C. Brown, ed., *The New International Dictionary of New Testament Theology* (Exeter: Paternoster Press, 1971), hereafter referred to as *NIDNTT*.

18. Gen. 32:27–30, Judg. 13:6, 17–19.

19. Exod. 6:2–8.

20. Bietenhard, in *NIDNTT.* There is a reference to J. D. Hyatt, *Exodus* (1971); Cf. *EDR,* s. v. "Name" and "God"; J. D. Goitein, "YHWH the Passionate: The Monotheistic Meaning and Origin of the Name YHWH," in *VT* 6(1956), 1–9; J. Miranda, *Marx and the Bible* (Maryknoll, N.Y.: Orbis Books, 1974).

21. Miranda, 294–96.

22. We may recall in this connection a verse from Nammāḷvar's *Tiruvaymoli,* 2.5.10: "He is not a male, He is not a female, He is not a neuter; He is not to be seen; He neither is nor is not; when He is sought, He will take the form in which He is sought, and again He will not come in such a form. It is indeed difficult to describe the nature of the Lord." Quoted in W. T. De Bary, ed., *Sources of Indian Tradition* (New York: Columbia University Press, 1958), 356.

23. *Māṇḍūkya Upanishad* 1–12, trans. R. C. Zaehner, *Hindu Scriptures* (London: Dent, 1968).

24. Ibid.

25. *Maitri Upanishad* 6.3–5.

26. Ibid. 6.23; *Kausitake Upanishad* 1.7.

27. Sat-cit-ānanda (reality or truth/mind or consciousness/bliss) become in combination saccidānanda. On ānanda see G. Gispert-Sauch, *The Concept of Ānanda in the Upanishads* (New Delhi: Oriental Publishers, 1977).

28. Abhishiktananda, *Saccidananda: A Christian Approach to Advaitic Experience* (Delhi: I.S.P.C.K., 1974), 167. Original French title: *Sagesse Hindoue, Mystique Chretiénne* (Paris: Centurion, 1965).

29. Samyadvāma, vāmāniḥ, bhāmaniḥ. *Chandogya Upanishad* 4.15, 2–4.

30. *Muṇḍaka Upanishad* 2.2, 1; 3.2.8.

31. *Maitri Up.* 7.1, 4, 6, 7.

32. Ibid. 5.2

33. *Bhāgavata Purāna* 2.4, 33, trans. G. V. Tagare, 5 vols. (Delhi: Motilal Banarsidass, 1976–78).

34. *Vāmana Purāṇa* 83.96–99.

35. Cf. *Bhāgavata Purāṇa* 6.2.14.

36. Quoted in De Bary, *Sources,* 347.

37. Lekh Raj Puri, *Radhaswami Teachings* (Beas, Punjab, 1972).

38. See M. Beardeau, *Theorie de la connaissance et Philosophie de la Parole dans le Brahmanisme Classique* (Paris: Mouton, 1964); P. Chakravarti, *The Linguistic Speculations of the Hindus* (Calcutta: University of Calcutta, 1933); Anandavardhana, *Dhvanyāloka,* ed. B. Bhattacharya (Calcutta: Firma K. L. Mukhopadhyaya, 1965); K. A. S. Iyer, *The Vākyapadiya of Bhartṛhari* (Delhi: Motilal Banarsidass, 1974).

39. Shobhārāni Basu, *Modern Indian Mysticism: A Comparative Critical Study,* 3 vols. (Varanasi: Bharat Sādhana Publications, 1974), 2: 160, hereafter referred to as *Mysticism.*

40. De Bary, *Sources,* 365–66.

41. I. Brianchaninov, *On the Jesus Prayer* (London: John M. Watkins, 1965); R. M. French, trans., *The Way of the Pilgrim and the Pilgrim Continues His Way* (New York: Seabury Press, 1965); a monk of the Eastern Church, *On the Invocation of the Name of Jesus* (London: The Fellowship of St. Alban and St. Sergius, 1970); a monk of the Eastern Church, *The Prayer of Jesus* (New York: Desclée, 1967).

42. Basu, *Mysticism,* 2:185, 241–42.

43. Ibid., 2:160–62, 572–73.

44. T. Bhaktivinode, *Nam-Bhajan* (Barnares: Viśwa-Vaiṣṇave-Rāja-Sabha, 1926), 13, 17–18.

45. Basu, 2:387–89, 391–95, 572–73, 162; Bhaktivinode, 25–26.

46. Panikkar, *MFH,* 259, 163, 260, 265.

47. Ibid., 272.

48. *Bṛhadāranyaka Upanishad.*, 2.3.6, 3.9.26, 4.2.4, 4.4.22, 4.5.15.

49. Ibid. 2.4.14, 3.8.11.

50. Puri, *Radhaswami Teachings*, 60–62, 71; Basu, *Mysticism*, 2.287–88.

51. *Bhagavad Gita* 10.38 (the whole chapter to be read in this connection).

52. *Maitri Up.* 6.22–23.

53. *Bhagavad Gita,* 2.52, cf. 11.8.

54. J. Hastings, *ERE,* 1917, s. v. "Name."

55. Clement of Alexandria, *Stromateis* 5.81f., trans. W. Wilson, Ante-Nicene Library Series, vol. 4 and 12 (Edinburgh: Clark, 1857).

56. Gregory Nazianzen, *Hymn to God,* PG 37, 507, quoted in Abhishiktananda, 1.

57. V. Lossky, *The Mystical Theology of the Eastern Church* (London: James Clark, 1944, 1957), 33–34. cf. *Kena Upanishad* 2.1–4 and 4.4; *Bhagavad Gita* 2.29.

58. T. Hopko, *EDR,* s. v. "apophatic."

59. Augustine *De Ordine* 2.16, 44; 18.47, "sciendo Deus ignoratur, nesciendo cognoscitur."

60. *The Cloud of Unknowing,* trans. C. Wolters (Harmondsworth, Eng.: Penguin Classics, 1961), chaps. 4 and 8, 55 and 65.

61. *Kaṭha Upanishad* 1.2.23; *Muṇḍaka Up.* 3.2.3, trans. S. Radhakrishnan.

62. *Bhagavad Gita* 11.48, cf. 11.53.

63. Ibid. 54.

64. *The Cloud of Unknowing,* chaps. 4 and 8.

65. *Kena Up.* 2.4.

66. Ibid. 4.4. Two different translations by S. Radhakrishnan and R. C. Zaehner. See the same idea of "a shaft of spiritual light piercing the cloud of unknowing" in *The Cloud of Unknowing,* chap. 26.

67. *Kena Up.* 3.3.1–12, 3.4.1.

68. For the fragrance of Brahman and its link with nature, cf. *Kauṣitaki-Brāhmana Up.* 1.5: "He comes to the tree Ilya and the fragrance of Brahman enters into him." Cf. *Gita* 7.9, Krishna as fragrance; 2 Cor. 2:14–16, the aroma of Christ and Christians.

69. *Chāndogya Up.* 4.4–9. See also 4.10 where a pupil is taught by the fires.

70. *Māṇḍūkya Up.* 1 and 2.

71. Cf. Panikkar, *MFH,* 264–65, 272.

72. John 14:6.

73. Cf. R. Panikkar, *The Intra-Religious Dialogue* (New York: Paulist Press, 1978), 91–93.

74. Matt. 6:26–29, John 15:1, 8:12–9:5, 14:6, Rev. 14:1.

75. Mic. 3.

76. Jer. 22:15–16.

77. Job. 42:5

2

Icon and Theon
ROLE OF IMAGINATION AND SYMBOL IN THE APPREHENSION OF TRANSCENDENCE
A. ROBERT CAPONIGRI

Omnis natura Deum loquitur

—Hugh of St. Victor

Omnis mundi creatura
quasi liber et pictura
nobis est et speculum

—Alain de Lille

To speak of God has ever been the loftiest aspiration of human utterance and, at the same time, the source of deepest frustration and despair. For to speak of God, of the divine, is to speak of the transcendent, of that numinous presence—at once *mysterium, tremendum* and *fascinans,* in Otto's oft-cited words—which lies beyond the horizon of humanity's ken but which calls to us imperiously to be recognized and adored. However, an impassible barrier seems to oppose itself to such utterance—a barrier, an impediment, imposed not from without, by an alien force, but arising from a profound inner source, constitutive of humanity's own consciousness.

The imperative drive of human consciousness is, of its own dynamism, toward immanence, that is, toward the total enclosure of all being, all reality within the horizon and the limits of consciousness. What presumably might fall beyond that horizon, those confines, is the naught, the unthinkable, the unutterable. To be is to be thought, to be thinkable (in the widest sense of these terms). This is the great immanentistic dogma which has laid hold on Western consciousness and created the indomitable "idealist." To this mode of consciousness the "problem" of God presents, ostensibly, a clear disjunction: either God must be brought within the horizon of thought, as in the great systems of Spinoza and Hegel, or he must be banished from the realm of the thinkable, that is, the real.

Still there is, withal, something in men and women which finally shrinks from such intransigent humanism. We are warned by an interior admonition as urgent as the daimon of Socrates that such humanism disguises an ultimately destructive hubris. We are warned by an admonition which evokes, however dimly, the haunting presence of that transcendent "other" which beckons us, as Wordsworth wrote, as a true home. Our deepest aspiration, more profound and insistently perturbing—the "inquiétude religieuse" of Bremond[1]—than this seductive humanistic urge, is to find a way to that transcendent haven. The problem of God, of thought and utterance about God, is to find a pathway to the transcendent.

Still, the humanistic thrust is strong enough to demand that this pathway—its initial aperture, its *terminus a quo*—at least be sought within the structure of human consciousness itself. The way of revelation from above, from beyond, is, of course, always a possibility. To deny the power of the transcendent to reveal itself, to speak to men and women of its own initiative, is contrary to the very notion of the transcendent. A mute God is the most inconceivable God of all. Should the transcendent so choose to speak and to reveal itself, its authority must, of necessity, be recognized as absolute.

Nevertheless, even granted these absolutes, there still lingers that which renders revelation, in this absolute sense, uncongenial to humanity: the contingency which attends it. Such revelation waits on a transcendent initiative—one not, therefore, within human compass and control. This contingency imparts to revelation a semblance of violence, invasion, and intrusion from without, which somehow seems a violation of human freedom and autonomy. Even more importantly, in this form revelation still leaves the transcendent, the absolute "other," which we—though we bow before it, though we harken to its words in awe, adoration, or simply fear and trembling—can never assimilate and embrace completely. The God of the Old Testament seems to illustrate this truth; he is an angry and jealous God. But more profoundly still, he is a frustrated God, for he feels this unbridgeable estrangement far more than those to whom he vouchsafes his revelation. Revelation, in this sense, seems to possess the power to assuage the hunger neither of the heart nor of the mind of humanity, and threatens to assume the status of idol and to make of humans the idolator. What we seek in our deepest religious longing is a sure path to the transcendent, the divine, from within our own being and consciousness. We seek a pathway within our own power and control, one arising from needs and longings we recognize as our own. We seek a passage which engages powers that are our own and which promises to invoke a transcendent presence which might assuage those needs and longings because, in some strange manner, we recognize in that transcendent presence not another, not an alien "other," but our own higher, truer self, to which we are returning.

But where within the domain of one's own conscious spirit, among its powers and resources, its poverty, its needs and aspirations, is such a pathway to be found? All those powers and resources, that wealth and that poverty alike, seem rather to drive humans toward enclosure, toward the ineluctable closure of the immanentistic circle from which all transcendent presence is excluded, from which there is "no exit," "*huis clos,*" in Sartre's pungent words. This conclusion seems inescapable, this plight fated, when one reflects upon the mode of operation of the two powers upon which Western men and women have most relied in their efforts to organize and structure, and hence render comprehensible the world of experience and access to and hold upon reality: sense and intellect. Sense and intellect alike appear, by their movement, to weave about humanity that tight cocoon of immanence within which we are enclosed, and which we profoundly long to transcend.

The effect of the senses in this direction seems the more readily apparent. This, despite the fact that the movement of the senses seems, at first glance, to lead humans in quite the opposite direction. It is they—sight, hearing, and touch—which first open consciousness upon the world, bring within its ken and compass the vast, surrounding world of form, sound, color, texture and taste. It is they which, in the first instance, break the terrible wall of closure within which, without them, the human spirit was quite literally imprisoned. The reading of that classic of the self-releasing power of the spirit, *The Story of My Life* by Helen Keller, with its grim struggle to force that breach upon the world against near adamantine obstacles, establishes this truth more immediately and convincingly than many learned tomes. Still, it is within this very movement toward aperture, out upon the world, that sense defines the limits of enclosure, of immanence. For the world which thus appears is the world which sense, the senses, delineate and define. In one same movement, they open the vista and close the horizon upon that world. The world which the senses reveal is at once inexhaustible and defined, humanity's prison and domain. "Nil . . . nisi prius in sensu . . ."

Within and upon this prison-world of sense, the powers of

human intellect are called into play. The intellect's mode of operation exhibits the same aspect of paradox as does the movement of the senses. In the first instance intellect appears as a vast power of expansion, of illumination, of aperture. It opens the world of ideas, of principles, of order within which the human soul moves with a freedom, a sense of mastery, of creative power ostensibly alien to the world of sense. It moves at the level of logic, of logical necessity, and achieves a lucidity and flexibility of language which endows it with a power of expression, reflection, and creative insight, which enables men and women to soar above that closed world of sense. All this is true to a degree; however, only to a degree, only within certain limits. The operation of intellect is in its turn limited, defined, confined. Its limits and confines are precisely those of the world of sense. Into this world intellect brings order, structure, penetration, control; always, however, within the limits defined by sense. Moving, as it is always strongly tempted to do, beyond those limits, to soar toward the transcendent, intellect loses contact with "reality," escapes into the world of ideal forms but leaves behind the concrete realm where men and women abide and act. The real power of intellect lies within the world of sense, to which, as has been noted, it imparts characteristics of highest value, but from which, no more than the senses, it can escape, and within which, with a stricture greater, perhaps, than that of sense, it encloses men and women. "Nichil in intellectu . . . nisi prius in sensu . . .," and while Leibniz hastens to add ". . . nisi intellectus ipse . . ." foreshadowing Kant, little consolation is forthcoming from his addendum unless it can be shown that further "nisi" is the signature of a real transcendent world.

Sense and intellect, however, powerful faculties though they are, do not exhaust the cognitive resources available to humans within the immanent domain of our own consciousness and spirit. A third power has always offered its succor to us; indeed, has always been powerfully active within consciousness—in ways, however, not clearly apprehended nor hospitably embraced, indeed, not infrequently, repulsed. This third power is *imagination*. It would not be too fanciful to suggest that the imagination has been—and, to a large extent, continues to be—the stepchild of the Western mind. Like the stepchild, the imagination is never entirely rejected, but never entirely embraced within the family; at times it is excessively denigrated, at others (under the goad, perhaps, of a nagging sense of guilt) excessively lauded. But above all, it is a never fully assessed power able, perhaps, to break the iron circle of immanence and to open a pathway to transcendence, to the divine, to God.

The Denigration of Imagination

Such an assessment of the imagination, given the cloud of ambiguity under which it has long suffered, must naturally take the form, initially at least, of an apology. Like any other apology, as Newman protested, this apology must begin with an identification, as clear as possible, of the allegation, or allegations, in which that ambiguity has its origin. In the case of the imagination, these allegations, or, at least, the radical one from which all others spring, are strong indeed. The imagination, that basic allegation reads, in Durand's words, "est rejetée comme la Maîtresse de l'erreur et de fausseté."[2] A harsher charge, it may be ventured, would be difficult to fabricate.

What, then, can be the cause of so harsh a judgment? That cause, as a matter of fact, proves to be not too difficult to point out. Durand, indeed, does so for us in lapidary form: "le triomphe du 'signe' sur le symbole" ("triumph of the 'sign' over the symbol"); and in another context, the exaltation of "direct" over "indirect" presentation of the world to human consciousness.[3]

The distinction between direct and indirect presentation is clearly the larger context for the more specific allegations. This distinction is supported by a very considerable and authoritative witness and consensus, though not eventually sustainable in sharp dichotomous form, as Langer, with others, points out.[4] The distinction is important because it provides the context for the "polarity" which Alquié develops in his valuable study between sign and symbol.[5] The distinction and interrelation of sign and symbol, in turn, similarly provide the context for the distinction and relation between letter and figure, literal and figurative expression, the literal and allusive modes of reference and interpretation. When this rather complex structure is reviewed, the ostensible ground of the indictment of the imagination, signalized above, may become clear enough to make evaluation of it and the indication of a viable alternative possible.

Consciousness, it has been averred, has at its disposition two modes or ways of representing the world to itself: the one "direct," the other "indirect."[6] In the first, the direct mode, the "thing" or "object" seems immediately, and in its own character, present to the mind; as examples, simple sensation and perception are ordinarily cited. The second, indirect mode, takes over when, for one reason or another, the "object" cannot present itself immediately, unmediatedly, "in flesh and bone," in Unamuno's phrase, to sensibility or perception. Examples of this contingency run a wide gamut, from simple matters of memory or recall, to the visions of science (as in the case of the movement of electrons about an atomic nucleus), to meditations of what might lie beyond death. The important point is that in all such instances of indirect knowledge the object in question, whether remembered scene or form, or scientific vision, or the visage of the hereafter, must be rendered mediately, by way of a process of mediation commonly designated as *re-presentation*. The agent of re-presentation is the imagination, its vehicle, the *image,* understood in this context and at this point in its widest, most inclusive and hence indeterminate sense.

The image, as this qualification suggests, it is not a fixed value. It is, rather, subject to modifications of degrees of re-presentational power. The measure of these degrees or modes is affirmed to be "adequation" to the object. Such "adequation" may be distributed along a projected continuum the extremes of which would be total commensuration (equivalent, it would seem, to direct presence, or only very feebly distinguished from it) or total incommensuration, absence. The most obvious example of this last is, of course, the divine, God. These distinctions must prove of great importance as the argument moves toward the problem of the transcendent and human access to it.

In the first case, that of commensuration, of near direct presence, the image, whatever its specific character, functions as a sign or even better as a signal, in Charles Morris' sense,[7] of the presence of the object. Expressed in another way, the object is merely "pointed to" or "warned of"; or again, it may be "verified," or experienced directly upon response to the signal. When, however, such commensuration, or proximation to immediate presence, or possibility of verification does not exist, when there is question of difficulty or impossibility of a reality of eventual direct presence, the image must function in another manner; it must "figure," that is, give sensible form to the reality in question. An innocuous example might be the effort to imagine what a prospective acquaintance whom one has never "seen" might "look like." In this latter instance we find ourselves in the presence of the image as "symbol"—a reality, as Shakespeare says of man, "of infinite variety" and, we might venture to add, even more difficult to decipher. These distinctions between direct presence and indirect, between sign and symbol, provide the context for such other distinctions as that between literal and figurative, discursive and presentational discourse. Literal utterance is utterance at the level or on the plane of direct presence, verifiable experience, the level of the sign; figurative utterance is utterance at the level, on the plane of, the symbol, in all its infinite variety; all further characterizations of discourse would seem to be subspecies of these.

The schematization seems entirely irenic; it contains no basic ground of discord which might lead to such harsh indictment of imagination as that mentioned above. The possibility of such indictment appears only when the question of "truth" arises and turns around the criterion of truth selected. In the indictment quoted: "imagination, the mistress of error and falsity" becomes comprehensible only when the sign, the "literal" utterance, characterized by the immediate presence, at least potentially through "verification" of the object (more precisely of the utterance) is taken as the criterion, the measure of the presence and normative form of truth. In this case the heavy charge "mistress of error and falsity" seems to fall with a certain naturalness upon the imagination and its figurative, symbolic works. Then the "triumph of sign over symbol" takes on significance and the process of the denigration of the imagination, under the rubric of truth, becomes plausible. The movement along the continuum between direct presence and total absence becomes, in this context, a process from truth to ever-deepening error and falsehood.

Described in this fashion, the denigration of the imagination and the symbol, of indirect presence and figurative utterance, the imputation to them of error and falsehood is only a possibility, an academic exercise. In fact, however, it would seem, and it has been seriously claimed and persuasively documented, that this imputation is no mere academic matter but historical fact. It constitutes, in fact, the authentic movement of the Western mind and the measure of its progress toward reality and enlightenment. Thus Langer almost poetically echoes, though not always faithfully, her masters Whitehead and Cassirer, who are on the whole more measured in utterance though no less decisive in final meaning and intent.[8] This movement, or drift, for it cannot be said to have been or to be entirely reflective or intentional, from indirect to direct, from figurative to literal, from symbol to sign, "the triumph of sign over symbol," marks the true history of the progress of the Western mind. If, as has surely been the case, it has involved in its movement the corresponding denigration of the imagination, of the symbol, of the figure, this cannot be considered regrettable except to those who cling, for whatever devious and not wholly calculable reasons, to stages of consciousness which the human mind, in the process of evolution and history, allegedly has transcended. To others, however, who think otherwise, this account of the movement of the human mind through history, its claim to constitute progress, arouses only skepticism; they see in it the historical denigration of the imagination whose movement has been traced in idea and the loss, through this denigration, of the most fecund resource of the human principal in its quest for that pathway to the transcendent which, as has been noted, is its most profound desire. For that movement toward alleged progress, they reserve the less honorific designation of "iconoclasm" and do not hesitate to define its stages.

Durand identifies the strongest and contemporaneously most effective current of this process of "iconoclasm" and the process of the denigration of symbol in favor of sign which is its heart, with Descartes and the Cartesian spirit which is the watershed of modern scientism. He writes: "La plus . . . dépréciation des symboles que nous présente l'histoire de notre civilisation est certainement celle qui se manifeste dans le courant scientiste issu du cartésianisme."[9] And Descartes is echoed in our own day by an epistemologist of otherwise decidedly un-cartesian bent, Bachelard, when he writes that the scientific mind and method must cleanse the object by a kind of "objective psychoanalysis" of all the deceptive associations with which the "imagination déformatrice" has laden it.[10]

The precise means by which Descartes effected this momentous change in the direction of Western thought and, it might be added, in the very concept of the optimal operation of the human mind, was the not too readily transparent, to lesser minds, dominance of the mathematical algorithm. This dominance did not carry with it, nor was it immediately supported by, any self-evidence. Pascal, a mind of equal mathematical perspicuity to that of Descartes, and a mystic of Catholic persuasion as well, denounced it. In this manner, Descartes secured that dominance of the sign over the symbol which is the bastion of the modern scientific mind. As Durand expresses the matter: "Le symbole—dont le significant n'a plus la diaphanité du signe—s'estompe peu à peu dans la pure sémiologie, s'évapore, pour ainsi dire, méthodiquement en signe."[11] The first intention of Descartes, it seems true, was to restrict the mathematical algorithm to the physical world. By the "je pense," however, he extended it to being itself. Thought, the mathematical method, thus becomes the only indication of being. The symbol is gradually resolved, "evaporates," in Durand's phrase,[12] into the pure sign. Descartes' followers, Malebranche and, above all, Spinoza, did not hesitate to extend this reductive method of analytic geometry to "absolute being," to God, the absolute "àu delá" resistent to all representation.

Most significantly, as the sequel will prove, Durand directs attention to the deleterious effect of this dominance of the sign over the symbol on art, whether painting or sculpture, though not so gravely, it would appear, on music. The artist, like the image, simple or iconic, no longer has a place in a society or culture which has, by degrees, eliminated the essential function of the symbolic image. After the great and symbolic allegories of the Renaissance, the art of succeeding periods declines more and more toward pure diversion, ornament, decoration, or meaningless "originality" and experimentalism. In Lebrun, David, Ingres, Léger, Chagall, Picasso, Mirò (I would offer de Chirico as an occasional exception) "le rôle de l'icone se reduit à celui du décor." Never again, perhaps, will the artist and art regain, in Western society, the powerful role and meaning which they exercised in "les societés iconophiles," for instance, now little esteemed Byzantium.[13]

Newton and Leibniz did indeed react against Descartes. Their reaction, however, proved as "iconoclastic," in the long run, as the method of Descartes. With them, in fact, began the reign of the method of analysis and mathematical measure, which led eventually to positivism in its many forms, which led to our own day, in which the denigration of imagination and symbol and the apotheosis of sign continue. Their continuation can be seen, for example, in Brunschvicg, who sees in imagination "le pêche contre l'esprit,"[14] ("the sin [of mind] against mind"); in Alain, who views it as the confused infancy of consciousness;[15] in Sartre, for whom "l'imaginaire" is the vehicle of the "naught" ("le néant"), the "phantom object."[16]

Like all else in history, the denigration of the imagination and the triumph of sign over symbol had exemplifications antecedent to Descartes, as they have had subsequently. We have no need for our present purpose to enter into the account of this rich history. We have only to note that just as there is a constant recurrence of the will "estomper le symbole" there is the constant recurrence, at crucial periods, to recover the symbol's power to open anew, in contemporaneously persuasive form, that pathway to transcendence which humans seek. Every indication testifies to the fact that the present is such a crucial time and points our concern to that recurrent need to see the imagination once more in its true character.

Imagination and Its Powers

As the denigration of the imagination has taken the form of its excoriation as "maîtresse de l'erreur" and as the "triumph of sign over symbol," thus closing the iron circle of immanence, so any vindication of the imagination must trace an inverse course. It must seek in the first place to establish the symbol in its power to reach truth and its power to do so in the process of opening the avenue for man to the transcendence, ultimately, to the *theon,* to the divine, to God. The following paragraphs will try to meet these objectives by advancing two propositions. The first proposition avers that the symbol, especially in its strongest form, the icon, achieves truth by revealing the absent object—that which in the distinction between "direct" and "indirect" modes cannot be present in the "direct," or, more precisely, permits the absent object to reveal itself in its own character and traits. The second proposition avers that the symbol can achieve or effect truth as self-revelation of the object because the proper mode of operation of the symbol is not "re-presentation," as Durand and his post-structuralist *confrères* suggest, but invocation, to which the epiphany of the transcendent in its proper, or in the case of God, its self-elected, traits or character is the response.

Some confusion, requiring clarification, seems to prevail among the concepts "sign," "literal," and "representation" as they come into play in the initial formulation of the problem of access to the transcendent. It is correct to assume as the norm of truth the direct presence of the object, in its own traits and character, to consciousness. In this sense the concept "literal" seems an axial concept to which other concepts are referable. It would seem, at the same time, an error, involved in the "triumph of sign over symbol," to assign to the "sign" the power of ensuring such direct presence. Thus arises the error involved in that process, remarked by Durand, by which "le symbole s'estompe dans la pure sémiologie"[17] under the impression that the sign possesses that "diaphanité" which insures that direct presence of the object in its proper traits. The sign possesses no such power and conveys no such assurance. Rather than diaphanous, it should be recognized as the most opaque of units, a mere "signal" as Morris points out,[18] in need of the most elaborate deciphering. Nevertheless, on the assumption of this diaphanous character, or at least while leaving this claim unchallenged, the process of representation is introduced as the alternative process for bringing all those objects which, for one reason or another, to cite Durand again,[19] are not subject to such direct presence and hence do not fall under the power of the sign. It becomes immediately apparent, however, that the process of representation can in no measure meet the criterion of truth as stated. Representation has no power to bring the "nonpresentable" object into presence in its own traits and character. Instead, it must have recourse to the system of the tropes. By the process of representation the symbol "s'estompe" not into the sign, but into the trope. The trope, however, in its turn has no power to bring the absent object into direct presence in its own terms and traits; nor, more importantly, does it advance any pretentions of doing so. The trope is not a remedial device called upon to compensate those situations in which the diaphanous sign does not operate. The tropes have quite a different office, that of generating an order of traits which the object does not possess but which serve to create an ambience of reference in which the authentic traits of the object take on intensified quality. Thus, to say of a maid that she is as fresh as a rose in bloom, is not to claim the property expressed by the trope as one proper to the girl but is to create an ambience of reference which places the proper qualities, or, more precisely, the specific proper quality which the trope addresses, in an intenser perceptual perspective. Indeed, it may, and must, be recognized that in its manner the trope does serve the norm of truth, namely, the rendering present of the object in its own traits; but this is not the direct office of the trope. Its direct office is the creation of the ambience of reference. For this reason representation cannot be regarded as adequately defining the mode of operation of the symbol.

Rather, what representation, left to its own devices, does is to create a surrogate of the absent object. This surrogate, in the nature of the case, can never fully "re-present" that object, or approximate its proper traits; it runs the risk, consequently, of producing a kind of parody of that absent object, a parody which in the case of the ultimate transcendent, the theon, God, runs the further risk of becoming an idol and making of man an idolator. Representation runs these risks by reason of its basic mode of procedure, which involves, fundamentally, a misguided interpretation and employment of the tropes. Representation, in this account, proceeds by "figuration," that is, the creation of the symbol. Figuration, the symbol, is in this account still dominated by the notion of the object as given, even though postulated as "absent." The function of the symbol then, in this account, is to create the figure, the surrogate of the absent object. It does so in terms which it derives from elements or features of objects the direct presence of which is actual or at least possible, which may be present, therefore, through the "diaphanité" of the sign. The representation of these features then, by recourse to one or another of the tropes, whose *corpus* has been established by classical poetics and rhetoric, ascribes to the absent object through its "figure," or "image." It is clear that in this process or procedure, the absent object can never be rendered present in its proper features. It comes before consciousness only "darkly," as "in a mirror," in St. Paul's words on our knowledge of God, with the inescapable if not constitutive tendency of the mirror to distort or to deform. Thus in this account humans are condemned to live and move in a twilight vision of the transcendent—above all of the *theon,* of the divine, of God.

This consequence of symbol as representation is no accident. It stems directly from the erroneous notion of the process of symbolization which constitutes the heart of the procedure of representation. In representation, the process of symbolization is projection. By recourse to the trope (erroneously conceived, as we have noted) the abstracted features of the immediately given or present are projected upon the immedicably, the constitutively absent, in a word, upon the void. No wonder Sartre, captured by this account of the movement of the imagination through the symbol, could only depict the realm of "l'imaginaire" as that of "néant," of "l'objet fantôme."[20] The rectification of this basic misconception of the process of symbolization is clearly, as a consequence, the crux of the matter. The process of symbolization is *not* projection. It is precisely the inverse. The process of symbolization is *invocation.* Only through the symbol as invocation can the transcendent be rendered present to consciousness in its own traits and features. It is this conception of "invocation" as the constitutive process of symbolization which must be clarified if humanity's pathway to the transcendent, ultimately to God, is to be assured. The clarification of the notion of symbol as "invocation" requires, however, as its prior condition, some further light on that of transcendence and the transcendent.

Transcendence is not an absolute concept. There is not an absolute, unbridgeable gulf between presence and absence, the same and the other, reality and appearance. On the contrary, the entire fabric of reality is woven of the intexture, the web and the woof (to recall the image so cherished, in its metaphysical implications, by George Eliot) of absence and presence, of the same and the other, in an infinitely subtle dialectic, as Plato strove to establish in the intricate argument of the *Sophist*. The locus of this dialectic is human consciousness. For human consciousness, all is potentially absence, all potentially other, all potentially the same. The human mind can even project the notion of its own absolute other, that is, a mind to which all would be absolute presence; immediately, however, it must recognize the fact that this absolute other, as absolute and as other, is yet not absence but presence, as the limit-image of its own dialectical movement. The reality of mind itself is the perpetual play of this dialectic by which it calls the absent into presence, the other into the unity of the same. Immanence and transcendence are thus seen to be the ultimate dialectical terms between which mind moves to weave reality. The ultimate question, consequently, is the nature, the constitutive character of this movement. This nature, this character, is invocation. Its medium or vehicle of realization is that product or expression of the image which we call symbol. And symbol and invocation are mutually defining terms. The whole meaning of symbol is the very process of invocation; the unique vehicle, or form of realization of invocation is the symbol in all its forms and degrees.

The essential movement of symbol as invocation is to call upon the transcendent to reveal itself in the medium of immanence, that is, in terms of consciousness itself. Thus mind, consciousness, as immanence, the locus of all presence, is essentially *openness* to the transcendent in all its forms and degrees. The symbol as invocation calls upon the transcendent to reveal itself, not in terms imposed by consciousness, but in the terms and features proper to the transcendent itself. In this way, the "iron circle" of immanence, with which, simply as a point of departure, our inquiry began, is broken; the essential relation of symbol to truth, that is, the presence of being to consciousness in its, that is, being's, own features, is established. Aperture to the transcendent is thus seen to be the very constitutive character of immanence, the pathway to the transcendent, the natural avenue of the commerce of consciousness.

Transcendence may be viewed, properly, in a number of ways; or, to express the same matter somewhat differently, is subject to degrees. In like manner the symbol and its constitutive procedure, its essence, really, invocation, exhibits a variety of forms or modalities which correspond with considerable faithfulness to the forms and degrees of transcendence. In the first instance, transcendence may be viewed as absence. Apparently, this designation of transcendence is negative; the designation as absence, however, is just and important, especially, as may appear, with respect to the divine, whose absence or hiddenness has become almost an axiom of religious thought. All absence, however negative it may appear, encloses a positive moment. It is this positive moment which distinguishes absence from the naught; and it was his frustration in seeking to discern this positive moment within absence that led Sartre to identify the core of the "imaginaire" as the "naught," "néant." The positive moment, which lies hidden at the heart of absence, is the power of the transcendent to respond to invocation, to reveal itself, or, in the case of the human person, to take the form and assume the traits which it elects. What is here said of the person is truest, of course, of the divine, of God, but with what difference must presently appear. (By way of parenthesis, it may here be remarked that in most theories of the person, especially those which take the form of "personalism," the tendency seems to be to emphasize the thrust toward revelation, toward presence to the other, and this is just. This must, however, be balanced by an equal or even greater emphasis on the hiddenness of the person which shelters its power of response to invocation, its capacity for self-revelation. For it is precisely in this hiddenness that its freedom, the highest mark of its status as person, resides. Moreover, it is this freedom, sheltered in hiddenness, which radically differentiates the person from nature; freedom in hiddenness makes it possible for the person to elect the mode of response and the degree and form of self-revelation, even, as both Augustine and, in his wake, Kierkegaard have noted, to the point of deception.) All that is here noted of the human person is applicable *mutatis mutandis* to God, save the capacity to deceive. The absolute veracity of the divine was correctly perceived by classical Christian theology, and even by Descartes for reasons of his own, and must of course figure in every reflection on the divine revelation. It is this positive moment of transcendence, its power to respond and the form that response may take, that invocation in the symbol addresses, and because of the variety, the capacity, and the possible election of response, invocation, and symbolization, becomes a form of exploration, of quest as it seeks to identify that capacity and disposition and to conform its own character to what it thus discovers.

The essential process of the imagination may best be called "imaging," the creation of the sensible surrogate of absent object. In no sense, in this context, can the image be conceived as the "imitation" or "copy" of the object. To conceive it so would be absurd, since the features of the absent object, the object not available in direct presence, are unknown, hence in no way can be "imitated" or "copied." Nevertheless, as we have already noted, this mode of operation of the imagination cannot be considered adequate. For in the image, the absent, the transcendent, is revealed or figured or rendered present, not in its proper traits or features, but in borrowed garb, composed on the basis of tropes; hence the transcendent or absent object is not rendered present in its transcendent features but the image is debased to the status of a surrogate wholly enclosed within immanence. The weakness of this mode of imagination is that it opens the avenue immediately to the dialectic of "yea" and "nay" in the image or symbol or figuration. To cite a gospel example, men and women should indeed have confidence that God cares for them as he does for the birds of the air; but men and women are not birds of the air. The "nay" which lurks in every image, figuration, or symbol at this level is indeed the avenue to an eventual charge of error, of deformation, even of falsehood as Durand, Brunschvicg and others have noted, to the charge that discourse about the absent, the transcendent in this vein can only involve men and women and their world in a web of illusion. What is thus symbolized or figured can never be present as it is in itself; still, such presence alone can satisfy the conditions of knowledge and truth. The goal, the office of imagination is to render the absent present in its own features, not in borrowed garb. Its aim, therefore is truth in no mitigated form. So, while indeed imagination may, at an inferior level, exercise itself in imaging, at its superior levels its procedure is quite diverse, not as imaging, but as we have noted, as invocation. In its operation as invocation imagination calls upon the absent, the transcendent to *reveal itself,* in response to invocation, in its own features and character, in those of its own election. The expression, or product, of the imagination at this level is not the image but the *icon*. As icon the imagination opens the avenue to the transcendent in authentic fashion, for it does not define, by oblique figuration through the tropes, the conditions under which the absent is rendered present, but invites, invokes and pleads, as in prayer, for the transcendent to reveal itself, to render itself present in its own terms.

This process of invocation, this realm of the icon is readily illustrated or exemplified at different levels and in different contexts of the imagination's activity. A ready example lies in the address to nature. The invocation of nature is an almost universal character of cultural life at every level. Anthropologists have explored this transaction at the level of so-called "primitive" cultures exhaustively. In the present case we may avail ourselves of an example from a more proximate context. Anyone acquainted with the "Lines Above Tintern Abbey" can only with difficulty miss the invocational tonality of those reflections. The poet calls upon nature to reveal itself to him and waits in inward silence for its response. And so it is with every sincere poet of nature. This address to nature is diametrically opposed to that of modern science, which dictates, through mathematics and experiment, the conditions under which nature is commanded to appear. As Bachelard writes "les axes de la science et de l'imaginaire sont d'abord inverses."[21] In another context it is recounted biographically of the famous art critic and connoisseur, Bernard Berenson, that his enrapture with nature was even more intense than his ecstatic response to art. In both instances, however, his attitude and disposition were identical: silent invocation, asking the one and the other, the scene of nature and the work of art, to reveal themselves to his expectant eye. Though so nearly identical, his invocational disposition before nature may appear to have been even deeper than that before the work of art, for it was nature which spoke to him most strongly of that transcendent presence to which he found it possible to apply only the highly inadequate epithet *IT*, but of the effective reality of which he never appeared to doubt.

The invocational character of imagination in the icon is even more readily and more forceably present in art, alike visual, verbal and plastic. It is not, of course, to be claimed that art in every instance achieves invocational status, the status of the icon, and even less that, to be accorded recognition as art, a work must achieve such status. As Berenson, and others with him, have pointed out, illustration, decoration, instruction, even diversion, are justifiable goals of artistic activity. Thus in his view, Raphael, in whom Berenson recognized a supreme illustrator, Benozzo di Lesa, whose brilliant decorative skill found expression in the *Procession of the Kings,* Botticelli, whose *Madonnas* are executed with consummate skill but remain pictorial withal, are art to a noble degree. But who would fail to see how sharply above these rise the *St. Francis* of Cimabue, the *Maestà,* or the *Calling of the Fishermen* of Duccio (so different in theme but so identical in iconic character), the *Annunciation* of Simone Martini.

And in what does this "above," a perilously invidious term, consist; what precisely does it signify? Nothing abstract, but something quite palpable, that is, their invocational and iconic character. In them one senses the response of the transcendent to the invocational appeal. In them it is the transcendent reality which appears, reveals itself in visible form: the voice which called to Francis from on high and transformed him, body, mind, and soul; the message of the Angel to Mary's receptive, but as yet not fully knowing soul, responding in faith, the ineffable elevation above all things natural of the Theotokos. These works are not representations, they are, one and all, icons, the *loci* of *epiphany* of the *transcendent* in its elected mode of self-revelation, powerful enough to bring their creators, the artists, to their knees in awed response to what the work of their hands and vision has called forth from beyond. It is in the great icons of Byzantine art that this iconic power, this epiphantic character is most universally recognized; it is to be felt as well, however, though in gentler vein, in such exquisite expressions as the *Good Shepherd* of St. Apollinare in Classe. Here, in the immanent structure of the work, line, mass, color, perspective, the epiphany of the transcendent transpires in response to the invocation of the artist. To his prayer in paint, the transcendent appears in the only way it can appear, by self-revelation in response to human appeal, never to human command. But the same characteristic is to be felt in stone as well. Who, gazing on the *Rondonini Pietà,* cannot all but hear the agonizing invocation to the mother of God to reveal the eternal and transcendent meaning of the life of the man-god, whose mortal remains she supports in fragile embrace, to make clear the meaning of that moment of celestial torment when she received that piteous sacred form from the hands of Arimathea. In that "unfinished" form, that agony is not represented by merely human vision but evinced and communicated in unforgettable epiphany, an appearance which the artist could never claim as merely his own. It is no invidious contrast to set the Rondonini side by side with the Petrine; the loveliness of the latter is surely everlasting. But it is Michelangelo who dictates the vision here, the transcendent, there. It is not to be concluded, as these examples might seem to suggest, that this iconic, invocational, epiphantic character is to be restricted to "religious" art. On the contrary, the transcendent, like the spirit, moves where it lists. Who can deny this character to depictions of purely "profane" or "secular" subjects, if such there really be? To a "Tempest" of Giorgione, to a Goya of the dark days, to de Chirico in his intenser moments? The latter's invocation, it is true, is directed, not to heaven, perhaps, but to the dim unconscious of the human "anima" which he calls upon to speak, and speak it does, in answer to his call.

Not to extend the inventory beyond staying power, it must, nevertheless, be placed in the record that there is ample evidence that the iconic form, the invocational-epiphantic character, informs the verbal idiom as well, whether poem, play or great fiction. This character appears clearly, for example, in the works of Tolstoy, making of them true icons, (though this deep trait seems to go unremarked by Berlin in his searching study) and not only in his "major" works, *Anna Karenina,* for example (in whose passion-flayed spirit, the eternal blasted womanhood surely appears); but *magnum in parvo,* the same quality appears in that perfect tale "The Death of Ivan Illych." In Ivan and his fate Tolstoy does not represent the death of a single man, but death itself which comes to every man, an implacable invader and not infrequently in humiliatingly trivial form—an insult to the ridiculously proud spirit of man— "just a fall, a little fall," but death, nevertheless. Work after work of poetry might be cited to this same effect in Leopardi: the *Infinite,* the *Last Song of Sappho;* in Petrarch: the *Triumphs,* which overcome essentially rhetorical occasions to evoke visions far beyond representation; in Wordsworth in his highest moments: *Tintern, Intimations,* the lyrical sonnet to Dorothy whose single line ". . . the difference to me . . . " speaks the ultimate loneliness in loss of every human soul; even in Tennyson, in those moments of *In Memoriam* in which his pleading spirit invokes—and receives—from the transcendent some intimation of the meaning of his friend's enigmatic death.

To distinguish the icon is not a facile undertaking or small accomplishment. It demands the invocational disposition in the auditor and the viewer as well as in the artist. But once that distinction has been made, the impression is indelible.

Though we have gone to some extreme to mark out the range of the icon, of invocation and epiphany in nature and in art, it is still true that it is in religion that this symbolic transaction is most fully realized, not only in the realm of the imagination but in the ontological and historical order as well. Most readily to be cited, of course, are the icons of Middle Eastern Christianity: Russian, Greek, and Balkan. The great Christs Pantocrator, to be found everywhere in the churches and monasteries of those regions, the haunting Virgins and Child, the figures of the Saints and of the events in the life of Christ, such as the Transfiguration, clearly bear the mark and deserve the designation of icon in the fullest sense of the term. The representational element in these works is reduced to a minimum; it is but the fragile sensuous medium or vehicle or locus, as one may prefer, of the transcendent presence which dwells in those icons and which comes forward to engage the viewer with the immediacy and power of personal encounter. The features of the subject send one at once, not to the personality of the artist, who is almost invariably anonymous, the unnamed voice and hand of invocation, but to the quality of the subject revealing itself—presenting, as does all real presence, at once immediacy and mystery in a union beyond resolution. One should note, in this context, how closely this iconic character has been approached in the great altar tapestry of the rebuilt, or rather entirely reconceived and executed, cathedral in Coventry—yet with a difference. The figure here moves more in the direction of representation and illustration; the quality of invocation and response is not absent, to be sure, but weakened and attenuated—evidence of the derivative character of the entire opus.

That invocation is closely allied to prayer; indeed, as has been pointed out with irrefutable force and clarity by Henri Bremond[22] and Romano Guardini,[23] it inevitably elides into prayer with the existential intensification of the imaginative event. This elision of invocation into prayer marks the path from the artistic to the existential and ontological arena of the icon. Invocation and response and epiphany belong, in the very first instance, to the ontological existential and historical sphere of religion, that is, of religion not as creed but as event. In this sphere, the icon is not a representation even to a minimal degree. It is an event, terrestrial and celestial, like the depictions of El Greco in which earth and heaven, divine and human event are brought into one seamless unity.

For the Christian, and for all historical religions (that is, not religions which occur as occasions in history, but those which, like Christianity and Judaism, are historical in structure, and are fundamentally, in their most intimate reality, historical events), the great icon event is the totality of salvation history, the entire event, in Judeo-Christian idiom, from creation to redemption and on to judgment and eternal disposition as anticipation, therefore, as fulfillment and continuation through historical time and beyond. In this idiom the invocational phase or dimension resides in the movement of salvation history from the fall to the advent of the Saviour. The Jewish people were the vehicle and voice of invocation, especially on the lips of the prophets whose office, as Newman states,[24] is essentially invocational. That entire phase of salvation is the appeal to God to reveal himself, not figuratively but historically. In this history both the acknowledgement of transcendence and the voice of invocation are present with equal force and emphasis; and wisely does the church retain within her advent liturgy the great hymn of invocation: Rorate coeli desuper / et nubes pluant justum.

In this historical perspective, Christ is the great icon. *He* is the response of the transcendent God to the invocation of mankind. And it is through Christ, as the great icon, that all that can be known about God is to be known, because Christ is the form in which the transcendent God elected to reveal himself. The ultimate and definitive pathway to the divine is by way of Christ and the whole knowledge of God is that available through Christ. "Who knows me, knows the Father."

There is every evidence in scripture and in church teaching that Christ knew himself fully in this role. His message to the disciples on the road to Emmaus (so movingly depicted by Rembrandt and many other artists in a number of media) expresses his understanding of his presence and office as the response of the transcendent to that historical invocation. Moreover, in Christ, the supreme icon, the complex structure of the icon is revealed. His very person bore this character in its very existence as a living icon in which the two basic aspects of icon meet and are established: response to invocation, and presence of the transcendent through its epiphany in the icon. The story of Christ's transfiguration is eminently designed to express this character—the immanence of the transcendent in the historical, existential form, revealed in a special light, for mankind, the light of faith. In every icon, as we have noted, so in Christ as icon, evidence and mystery are co-present. This paradoxical unity or unification is evidenced in Christ's own preoccupation with achieving a deeper and clearer understanding of himself. He is constantly seeking to clarify the manner in which the Father is revealed in him and the manner in which this epiphany is to be communicated to those for whom it is eventually intended. He comes to understand this last, with great agony, in the prayer in Gethsemane—namely, that it is through his death and resurrection that this great saving presence is to be communicated and perpetuated. Again, as the icon of salvation, he presents to his followers a constant problem in hermeneutics, so to say. They are constantly concerned to decipher his character, not infrequently stumble in the effort, and to the very end exhibit shadowy regions in the understanding they have achieved. The two lines of quest for light, his own and theirs, are brought into common focus when he demands of them in quite unvarnished terms "Whom do men say that I am? Whom do you say that I am?" He is seeking, in its reflection in others, a deeper understanding of himself. An older teaching held the view that Christ always enjoyed full and perfect self-knowledge; this persuasion seems, however, not in entire conformity with the incarnation with his truly human character and reality. For humanity's self-knowledge is always a seeking; in Christ's instance it takes the special form of the quest of the Godhead, of the transcendent in himself as the key to his own real identity.

The iconic character of Christ and his mission is continued in the world and in history in the church and its sacraments. Quite rightly the church has been called the "mystical body" of Christ. For its being is not one separate and distinct from his; but the continuation of his own. This continuation is established, in the first instance, by his resurrection, which here finds one of the most profound dimensions of its meaning. A central part of the resurrection is precisely the continuation of his life in the church after death and burial. The church is part of the meaning of the empty tomb. It too enjoys the status of icon, which is exhibited even in its incarnation in institutional form in the movement of history. This institutional form— one of the most misapprehended and severely excoriated aspects of the church's being—also has symbolic force. From one point of view its origin and life can be construed in terms of the processes common to all human institutions, just as Christ's own life fulfilled the human cycle of birth, activity, and death. To faith, however, the very existence of the church through time and history is a perpetual transfiguration through which the continuation of his life is manifested.

The same truth is manifested in the church's sacraments. These have many of the incarnational traits, which are described in purely "natural," even evolutionary terms by anthropologists. But through them moves the same lifegiving and redeeming power which awakened the young girl from her sleep in death, answered the centurion's behest, and summoned Lazarus forth in his burial shroud. This iconic character is revealed most clearly in Christ's own sacrament, as it has been called, the Eucharist. The essential moment of the ritual of this sacrament is invocational—the hands of the celebrant extended over the host and chalice as he invokes God's transforming power upon them through the ritual repetition of Christ's own instituting words. The iconic character is fulfilled, finally, in the manner in which the communicants in church and sacraments take on the life of which these are the continuators and communicators, that is, the life of God through Christ.

In the icon, and the complex processes it embraces, there is to be found that triumph of symbol over sign which is the highest work of imagination and the "reversal," in the sense this term has in reference to ancient epic and tragedy, of its denigration. Far from teacher of error and falsehood, imagination becomes, in the icon, in all its forms and range, but above all in religion, the carrier of the highest truth: the epiphany of the transcendent, the *theon,* God in the matrix of immanence.

NOTES

1. Henri Bremond, *L'inquiétude religieuse* (Paris: Perrin et Cie., 1924), series 1 and 2.

2. Gilbert Durand, *L'imagination symbolique* (Paris: Presses universitaires de France, 1964), 22: "L'imagination . . . est rejetée par tous les cartésiens comme la maîtresse de l'erreur."

3. Durand, 24: "Le cartésianisme assure le triomphe de l'iconoclasme . . . le triomphe du signe sur le symbole."

4. For the distinction between "direct" and "indirect" representation cf. Durand, 7: "La conscience dispose de deux manières pour se représenter le monde.

L'une *direct,* dans laquelle la chose elle-même semble présent à l'esprit . . .
L'autre *indirect* lorsque . . . la chose ne peut se présenter en chair et os à la
sensibilité . . ." The phrase "en chair et en os" is Unamuno's "carne y hueso";
cf. Miguel Unamuno, *Del sentimiento tragico de la vida en los hombres y en los
pueblos,* 4th ed. (Madrid: Editorial Renacimiento, n.d., chap. 2). For Langer's
reservation cf. Susanne K. Langer, *Philosophy in a New Key,* 3d. ed.
(Cambridge: Harvard University Press, 1969), chaps. 2 and 3.

5. F. Alguié, "Conscience et signe dans la philosophie moderne et le cartésianisme," in *Polarité du symbole,* Etudes carmélitaines (Paris: Desclée, 1960),
221ff.

6. Cf. Durand, Unamuno, and Langer.

7. Charles Morris, *Signs, Language and Behaviour,* in *Writings on the General Theory
of Signs* (The Hague: Mouton, 1971), esp. 100–103. Cf. Langer, preface to 1951
ed.

8. Langer, chap. 10, esp. 272ff.

9. Durand, 23.

10. Gaston Bachelard, *La formation de l'esprit scientifique: Contribution à une psycha-
nalyse de la connaissance objective* (Paris: n.p., 1938), Introduction.

11. Durand, 24.

12. Durand, 1,s.v. "s'évapore."

13. Durand, 26–27. As examples of "societés iconophiles" he cites Byzantium and
China of the Sung dynasty.

14. Leon Brunschvicg, *Héritage de mots, héritage d'idées* (Paris: n.p., 1945), 97–98.

15. Alain [Emile-Auguste Chartier], *Esquisses d'Alain* (Paris: n.p., 1963),
Préliminaires à la mythologie, 88ff.

16. Jean-Paul Sartre, *L'imaginaire: psychologie phénoménologique de l'imagination*
(Paris: n.p., 1940), 82ff., 174–75.

17. Durand, 24: "Le symbol . . . s'estompe peu à peu dans la sémiologie."

18. Morris.

19. Cf. Durand, Unamuno, and Langer.

20. Cf. Sartre.

21. Bachelard, 68.

22. Cf. Henri Bremond, *Prière et poésie* (Paris: n.p., 1926).

23. Cf. Romano Guardini, *Über das Wesen des Kunstwerks,* 2d ed. (Tübingen: n.p.,
1959), and *Sprache-Dichtung-Deutung* (Wurzburg, 1962).

24. Cf. John Henry Newman, *Lectures on the Prophetic Office of the Church* (Oxford:
J. H. Parker, 1837).

3

The Relationship Between Symbolic and Literal Language About God

FREDERICK M. JELLY

In his paper entitled "Does the Notion of 'Mystery'—As Another Name for God—Provide a Basis for a Dialogical Encounter between the Religions?" Heinrich Ott applies the notions of mystery found in the works of Rudolf Otto and Karl Rahner.[1] He responds positively to his own question: "Thus this notion of mystery which refers us to the superrational (not the antirational!) and to the inexpressible (not the speechless!), is in itself a guarantee that it cannot be misused as a new superstructure that would violate the openness of dialogue."[2] Armed with the conviction that we are all touched by the same mystery, as partners in this dialogue we are open to one another's insights from our own distinct religious experiences. In order to share such insights we must use our languages about God very carefully.

I propose to pursue a strand of thought left open by Ott's paper, namely, the exploration of linguistic usages in God-talk that might reconcile reasonable speech about divinity with the suprarational and inexpressible character of mystery. Without in any way indulging in the self-contradictory attempt to capture the meaning of mystery entirely, is there a language about God, or better, is there a possible combination of languages about ultimate reality which both preserves its transcendence and, at the very same time, also immanently grounds it in our experience? More precisely, what might be the cognitive content, if any, communicated by this combination of religious and theological languages, or is it impossible to expect human language to reveal any reflection of the divine reality? Is the most that we can hope to know about our God in this life—and so hope to share in our dialogue with each other—the affective and conative dimensions of our religious experience, so that the only cognitive content in our languages about ultimate reality would be a description of how we go about loving, honoring and serving our God, and what set of values our God has inspired in our hearts so that we may be properly motivated to love and serve our neighbor? Although such languages would be describing our religious relationships with our God as well as their impact upon our relationships with other human beings, such speech would be saying nothing really about ultimate reality which we encounter or the mystery that touches each one of us. What meaning do we assign to the names and concepts of Deity? It is our God of whom we are speaking and not just of ourselves in relationship with God, although these relationships in our religious experiences are essential in the revelation of ultimate reality to us. How can we share with each other dialogically unless there is some cognitive content in our languages about the One who is the very subject of our speech together?

My purpose, therefore, is to show that a dialectical relationship between our symbolic speech and our literal language about God seems well suited to the expression of both divine transcendence and immanence through our religious and theological languages. I describe the relationship between the symbolic and the literal in our God-talk as dialectical to communicate my conviction that our languages about ultimate reality cannot be either one or the other (just what "symbolic" and "literal" mean in the context of this essay will be explained at length). One without the other appears to terminate inevitably in erroneous extremes: the "symbolic" without the realistic grounding of the "literal" in some form of agnosticism of even atheism; the "literal" without the "symbolic" in an anthropomorphic interpretation. A doctrine of analogy will be proposed as mediating between the two poles in this dialectical relationship so that neither does the discourse about the inexpressible remove the mystery nor does the superrational character of the mystery become antirational by reducing our God-talk to nonsense as devoid of any cognitive content or meaning about ultimate reality itself. The distinction between "religious" and "theological" languages signifies that between first-order religious communication, e.g., of preaching, and second-order analysis of religious language in the interpretations of the theologian. This essay is intended to provide a theological analysis of the dialectical relationship between religious symbols and properly literal analogues in our languages about ultimate reality, with a view toward pursuing the question posed by Ott's paper. We might put the question this way: How do both symbolic speech and literal language about God help build upon the notion of mystery—another name for God—as a basis for a dialogical encounter between the religions?

Symbolic Speech About Ultimate Reality

In this type of God-talk we think of myths, metaphors, and images, as well as of religious symbols. Using John Macquarrie's work as our principal guide, let us carefully distinguish symbols from both myths and metaphors.[3] It is important to note that the following distinctions, as all valid distinctions, are to relate and not to isolate the entities and intentionalities involved. For a clearer communication we must indicate in what senses our words are being used so that they might come together in a context of sentences, paragraphs, and the written work as a whole in some sort of synthesis that coherently unifies the analysis. And, especially when considering the profound, indeed infinite, realities expressed in religious language, our human minds want to be as clear as possible about meanings and aspects of the mystery.

By the term *images* is meant in this essay a generic notion that applies to every sort of pictorial language, whether expressed in myths, symbols or metaphors. And so the immediate task before us is to distinguish religious symbols from both myths and metaphors. Even in its widest meaning, symbolic speech differs from myths which do not consciously distinguish symbols from what they symbolize. Mythology, which is proper to the religious experience of a people in its primitive stages, is a dramatic, evocative sort of story about a community's origins and destinies, its ultimate meaning and values, that draws no distinction between the literal and the symbolic. Myths are characterized by a state of immediacy and wholeness unbroken by the distinctions of analytical thinking.[4] Although the Bible for the most part completely abandoned unbroken myths, mythical elements did survive in the creation and flood stories of the Old Testament, as well as temptations of the Lord and the transfiguration incident of the New Testament. In a post-mythical age such as ours, the myth gets broken; its symbols are recognized as such and are interpreted existentially, i.e., in reference to what they symbolize for human existence in its totality or ultimate concerns, to use Paul Tillich's expression. Let us immediately take note of the fact that this process of "demythologizing" does not discard the symbols as no longer useful since they do not retain a great evocative power in the expression of religious experience. But they are no longer taken literally as in the mythical stage. All this does not mean that the myth is meaningless in our post-mythical age. For, as mythical elements survived even after myths were broken in the inspired sacred Scriptures of the Judeo-Christian tradition, so too do they persist, at least partially, into modern times. They remain a fertile source and important matrix for religious symbols; and as partners in a dialogue between the great religions of the world we must be especially conscious of their contribution to the religious experiences in the faiths of each one of us. The broken myth, therefore, does not lose its significance for us even *qua* myth, since it continues to nourish the evocative power of our religious symbols.

Likewise, the distinction between symbols and metaphors must be seen in proper perspective. The term *metaphor* is used primarily to designate a figure of speech in literary contexts. As poetic images, metaphors are designed to directly induce in us an aesthetic experience. Symbols, on the other hand, in the context of our consideration, are intended to elicit a religious response from us. Both, however, do focus our perception upon certain aspects of a reality or situation so that we do respond, whether with a religious or an esthetic experience. Now, since the religious dimension of our human experience is not just another aspect, not even the highest, but one that permeates and gives ultimacy to all other aspects, the sense of the beautiful evoked by metaphors may contribute to our sense of the numinous in our encounter with mystery or holy being. It is indeed evident from Holy Writ that many metaphors, figures of speech, and literary genres do enrich those special words and expressions that have emerged as symbols of faith in the strict sense. And so we have tried to show that symbols are not only distinct from myths and metaphors, but that, paradoxically, our very awareness of such differences enables us to perceive their interrelationship in the world of religious discourse.

In order to make more precise the meaning of religious symbols in this essay, it would be helpful at this point to clarify how they might be distinct from and related to "analogues." As the introduction to this essay has already indicated, a doctrine of analogy will be explained in some detail in the proper contexts of defining what is meant by *literal* language about God, and how it is to be dialectically related to symbolic speech about ultimate reality. Verbal symbols, with which we are concerned in contrast to such symbols as flags, emblems, etc., may be described as "words which stand for a thing or phenomenon which is itself a symbol, in so far as it stands for something else; so that the word, in such a case, refers indirectly through its immediate referend to whatever this may symbolize."[5] Jesus Christ is called "the true light that enlightens every man" in the prologue to the Fourth Gospel, and "Light from Light" in the Nicene Creed. In each case the language is symbolic, i.e., the words are verbal symbols or symbolic speech about God in Jesus Christ. In addition, moreover, light as a reality is looked upon as a symbol of divinity. While the words immediately refer to the phenomenon of light, they refer indirectly through their immediate referend, in the context of the Scriptures and the creed or in the universe of discourse where they are used, to the mystery of Christ's divinity, which light symbolizes.

According to Macquarrie, the difference between symbols and analogues "is that the best analogues are almost self-interpreting, whereas symbols frequently require much explanation of background before we begin to see where they are pointing."[6] There seems to be a certain universality about analogues lacking in religious symbols which, even though well known, are derived from the historical background of a particular community. This difference would appear to be of special significance for our dialogue between the religions of the world, which indeed is made possible only through a certain universality of discourse. Such a universality of analogy seems to be based upon a more profound difference between analogues and symbols, i.e., the intrinsic likeness between the analogue and that for which it stands. Thus there seems to be some intrinsic likeness, similarity, or proportion (*analogy*) between human fatherhood and the fatherhood of God. Without pushing the comparison too far—to the point of likeness in every respect or a quasi-identity—the relationship of God to his creatures is not unlike the parent-child relationship. The parent-child relationship, which is universally known in human experience, provides an analogy of our relationship with God that is almost self-interpreting. The difficulties with regard to the experiences of the child who has never known the love of a human parent, or the inevitable imperfections found in human fatherhood, especially in a sinful humanity, do not invalidate this relationship's power to say something meaningful and true about God, not only in relation to us, but about his own reality as the source and exemplar of all fatherhood. But how are we to interpret this "intrinsic likeness" between the analogue of human paternity and the reality that it represents, divine fatherhood? Is it possible for the human intelligence to form a concept about God that leads to a literal, though extremely limited, language about God? And, if this be possible, how does it not dissolve the mystery of God, which ever remains beyond human speech and comprehension?

Literal Language About Ultimate Reality— Is It Really Possible?

At this juncture we might well pause for a moment to reflect upon the distinctions just drawn between religious symbols and analogues. Are the criteria proposed by Macquarrie sufficient to clarify the differences? He himself finds that they become blurred in the case of such symbols as water, which has a universal intrinsic symbolic power as representative of cleansing, and light, which bears some likeness to certain aspects of the Deity.[7] And so we now explore the problem of analogy further to clear up the matter as much as possible. But first allow me to add a note here: it is to impress upon the reader that my intent in this relatively brief essay is more to raise questions than to settle them, even though I do take some definite stands for the sake of stimulating a response.

"Literal" in this essay is the designation of the primary meaning of words as used in the particular context of a universe of discourse, which is religious language or theological language in our dialogue. And so it refers to speech in which words are not being employed in their extended meanings, such as the figurative senses in similes and metaphors or the symbolic significance of myths, allegories, parables, etc. Literal language, in other words, is nonsymbolic speech. Lion, for instance, primarily stands for the animal, and metaphorically can mean a man of great courage, as Christ, "the lion of Judah." Because there is frequently a confusion in the matter, especially in the context of God-talk, I would like to point out clearly that literal language does not always necessarily refer to realities and experiences that are empirically verifiable. For example, liberty as the quality in our human nature whereby we can choose, make decisions, etc., is not, as such or *qua* quality, empirically verifiable, as are realities directly perceptible to our senses. Freedom, however, does manfifest itself sensibly in our words and deeds. This does not reduce it to a purely sensible phenomenon. I am trying to make this clarification as carefully as possible since so much of the misunderstanding over the appropriateness of literal language predicated of God seems to stem from identifying it solely with objects perceptible to the senses. While the theory of knowledge called "moderate realism," particularly in the thomistic tradition, is based upon the principle that there is nothing in our intellectual understanding that does not first enter through sense experience, this in no way limits our concepts to material entities, since immaterial or spiritual realities can be known through their sensible effects and by way of analogy with them.

In our approach to the understanding of God, infinite Spirit—suprarational or superintelligible by reason both of his infinity and his immateriality—we must ever be aware of the inherent limitations of our human knowledge. St. Thomas Aquinas clearly taught that in this life ". . . we cannot know what God is, but only what he is not . . ."[8] In his initial approach to knowing God, he emphasized this *via negativa* which cleared away the misconceptions about ultimate reality which could cause confusion of the Creator with his creatures. It was, however, only the first step in his approach toward a very limited but literal and true understanding of ultimate reality. After proceeding to deny God of any composition whatsoever (even that of essence and existence in his subsistent being), any imperfection or lack of goodness as a transcendental property of being, any finitude whatsoever or limitation to space (ubiquity) and in time (eternity), as capable of any developmental change (immutability) and multiplicity (unicity), the Angelic Doctrine invoked another way, the *via eminentiae,* which attributes to ultimate reality pure perfections analogically, i.e., certain qualities found in creatures and to be predicated of God in a supereminent mode divested of all limitation.[9] Such perfections as being and its transcendental properties of truth, goodness, and beauty, as well as justice and mercy, are called pure, since they do not necessarily connote imperfection as do such mixed or alloyed perfections as corporeality, which must mean limitations of time and space, etc. We can, therefore, speak in a literal but definitely limited mode about divine being, truth, goodness, beauty, justice, mercy, etc. When we attribute these qualities to God *via eminentiae* analogically, the *via negativa* is still somewhat operative in the sense that we do negate the limitations in which they inherently exist within creatures. Consequently, while they do not necessarily imply imperfection essentially, existentially, in our human experience, which can only encounter creatures directly, they must be found in a finite state. If these positive perfections can be affirmed literally of God, they are still more unlike the ultimate reality than like it, which preserves the transcendence and incomprehensibility of the divine mystery, and avoids a naive anthropomorphism and fideistic religiosity. At the same time, this sort of analogical attribution does manage to prevent the opposing extremes of agnosticism and atheism because it does reflect some understanding of the divine Being that can ground our relationships with our God, who is also immanent to us. Macquarrie sums up most of what has been asserted here quite nicely:

The use of likenesses or similes was early seized upon in religious talk so as to stretch everyday language in such a way that it might—so it was hoped—embrace the gods, at least in some manner. This way of talking eventually developed into a full-blown doctrine of analogy, much discussed and elaborated in the Middle Ages. Thus the *via negationis* is supplemented by the *via eminentiae*. Both ways contrast the infinite with the finite, or creative Being with creaturely being, but whereas the *via negativa* simply denies the infinite all characteristics of the finite, the *via eminentiae* claims that every positive characteristic of the finite bears some affinity to a corresponding characteristic of the infinite, in which, so to speak, the positive characteristics of finite being are raised to a pre-eminent degree. *Thus every analogous predication involved the assertion both of likeness and unlikeness* [italics mine]. The possibility which this way offers of talking about God clearly depends on just how wide the gulf between God and created beings is taken to be, and on just how far language can be stretched without coming to a breaking point.[10]

Here some further precisions are called for. The pure perfections of which we have spoken are also to be distinguished from names and concepts of the Deity which designate relationships between God and us, such as Lord and Creator. Literal language about ultimate reality in our context strives to say something about God's perfections as properly his own, and not just that the divine creativity exercises some causal influence upon our perfections. At the same time, it is only the creaturely perfections that are *per se* pure, and particularly to be found in human persons made to the image and likeness of the triune God revealed in Jesus Christ, e.g., wisdom, love, etc., which are to be attributed to God as naming what the ultimate reality is in itself.

The very possibility of this sort of analogical predication does depend partially upon divine causality as efficient or communicating to creatures a limited share in the infinite perfections of the Deity, and partially upon the notion of likeness or participation by the creature which is in the order of exemplar causality. The crucial question before us is the nature of this ontological likeness. Is it truly, literally, and properly revelatory of what is intrinsic to the divine reality? It is significant to note in this context the reply that St. Thomas Aquinas gave to his own question, "Can we say anything literally about God?"

... God is known from the perfections that flow from him and are to be found in creatures yet which exist in him in a transcendent way. We understand such perfections, however, as we find them in creatures, and as we understand them so we use words to speak of them. We have to consider two things, therefore, in the words we use to attribute perfections to God, firstly the perfections themselves that are signified—goodness, life and the like—and secondly the way in which they are signified. So far as the perfections signified are concerned the words are used literally of God, and in fact more appropriately than they are used of creatures, for these perfections belong primarily to God and only secondarily to others. But so far as the way of signifying these perfections is concerned the words are used inappropriately, for they have a way of signifying that is appropriate to creatures.[11]

Contemporary thomists appeal to the authority of the *Doctor Communis* here and in many other places for a theological theory of analogy called analogy of intrinsic attribution.[12] This is an attempt to show how reason—even enlightened by God's revealing word and the grace of faith, which does not vitiate the natural process of human understanding—can come to know God's inner reality, truly but dimly in this life. As the great Anglican thomist, E. Mascall, has put it: "Here indeed we see as in a glass, darkly, and not yet face to face; nevertheless, we see."[13] Schematically, this theory of intrinsic attribution tries to combine features of the analogy of proper proportionality and the analogy of attribution based upon an extrinsic denomination. The classical example of the latter is health, as attributed to a human being or animal and to such secondary analogues as food, climate, and complexion. What is signified by "health," something like the harmonious condition of a living organism, can be predicated literally and intrinsically only of the prime analogate, a human or an animal, and of food and climate only insofar as they are conducive to good health or to complexion, as a sign of it. The perfection signified, therefore, is found intrinsically only in the primary analogue, and by extrinsic denomination in the secondary analogues. If we were to apply this kind of analogy to our understanding of God, we should not be getting beyond a description of our relationships to ultimate reality, whether that description be symbolic or not, and our names and concepts would express no intrinsically cognitive content about the Deity's own being. On the other hand, the analogy of proper proportionality, e.g., knowing as predicated of sense perception and intellectual understanding, does attribute a likeness to both analogues that is intrinsic. What is signified by the *ratio analogiata* of knowing, an identity in the psychic order between subject and object, is verified intrinsically by both sensation and intellection, even though in the latter in a vastly superior mode. Both forms of knowledge, however, are logically the inferiors of a generic notion of knowledge, the *ratio analogata*. If we were to apply this type of analogy to our understanding of God, then ultimate reality itself would become subject to such supreme genera as *ens in communi* (being in common) or *bonum in communi* (the transcendental property of goodness), etc., which would then embrace God as uncreated being and goodness, and creatures as finite participants in these pure perfections created in them by God. The error involved here is the construction of a logical genus that transcends being itself, goodness itself, etc. And so the theological theory of the analogy of intrinsic attribution seeks to name the Deity as the Prime Analogate transcending any generic classification in which the fullness of the pure perfection is found and in which fullness the creatures or secondary analogues participate in greater or lesser degree, but in whom the pure perfection does exist intrinsically, albeit in a finite mode. St. Thomas Aquinas can say, therefore, that the pure perfection is attributed literally to God, "and in fact more appropriately than they are used of creatures." For God is each one of these perfections in absolute simplicity, e.g., divine justice is really divine mercy in the plentitude of holy being itself. But, we must always recognize that our names and concepts have been derived from our experiences of such perfections as they actually exist in us and in our fellow creatures . This distinction, while preserving the transcendence of divine mystery, does not invalidate the truth of our literal language about God. To respond to my own question, posed as part of the title for this section of the essay, literal language about ultimate reality is possible, since the likeness between the Prime Analogate of Deity and the secondary analogues of creatures as participating in the divine fullness of pure perfection is intrinsic and so revelatory, ever so dimly, of God's own inner being itself. This is not to attribute a representational significance to our ideas about divinity, since they are always circumscribed by our finite experience; but it is to say that they can be nonsymbolic pointers to being itself, making possible for us an authentic knowledge of God.

Symbolic and Literal God-Talk and the Dialogue Between Religions

As stated at the outset, the primary purpose of this essay has been to distinguish carefully between the two religious and theological languages, that of symbols and analogues, in order to relate them dialectically as a better basis for interfaith dialogue. The fact that I devoted so much time to proper analogy and literal predictions about the Deity is not to be interpreted as meaning that such religious language is always to be preferred in our naming God. Each form of God-talk has its own proper place, and only a certain combination of both can achieve a balance in our discourse about the divinity and all that linguisticality implies for our religious experience as a whole.

Religious symbols, obviously, are endowed with an evocative power that summons a response from the total personality, the affective and conative dimensions, as well as the cognitive. They appear to be particularly powerful when interpreted existentially, i.e., as applied to the meaning of authentic human existence. For then their relevance to the commitment and values required by every religion is made more manifest and even more motivating. Were we ever tempted to dismiss them as useless or even as obstacles to our true understanding of our God, indeed our worship would become quite empty and our religious life would generally run the risk of being reduced to a sterile intellectualism.

On the other hand, if our approach to the Deity is pan-symbolic, and there is room for no other type of language in our discourse with and about the divine, then a number of undesirable effects can take place in our religious existence. What can the extended meanings of symbols really signify to us unless they can be grounded from time to time in a literal language more directly related to our daily experience. We are likely to make of religion a realm of fantasy removed from the realities of this world if there is insufficient cognitive support to our religious affections and aspirations. The very realism of ultimate reality gradually recedes. This is a danger especially indigenous to a secularized world such as ours, where religion is already separated from temporal affairs to the point of not being allowed to influence them. Surely I am not decrying the proper separation of church and state, nor am I decrying a genuine spirit of secularity in which we allow the world to be itself. Rather, I am emphasizing the fact that especially in such a society there must be a sound conviction about the reality of God's immanence in the world if we are to avoid the ideology of secularism which has sought, and still does, to outlaw the influence of all religious convictions and moral values in the public forum.

The absence of any acceptance of valid God-talk as revealing of the inner life of the mystery which touches us all can be destructive of dialogue both within a religious community and between religions. How can there be any authentic basic unity of faith without the cognitive content of a common creed that directs cult and code in the worship and commitments of a church or religion? How can we presume to indulge in a dialogue about God-talk here, as representatives of many religious and theological traditions, unless somehow we can share experiences that are intelligible to one another! And I submit that the proper and judicious use of literal language about God, particularly as carefully nuanced by the analogy of intrinsic attribution, is a necessary way of making our various symbols and myths meaningful to one another. We shall never experience the mutual enrichment of such understanding and openness in dialogue if it is impossible to share insights because our speaking languages are much more profoundly different than are diverse tongues. Let us prayerfully avoid the babbling of the Tower of Babel and reach up for the enlightenment and inspiration of the Pentecostal Spirit, the gift of tongues understandable to all who wish to proclaim the mighty deeds of God in our midst.

The existential interpretation of religious symbols in our various religions arising out of such a rich diversity of cultures, as significant as it has been for the rejuvenation of our faiths, still does not seem sufficient for the task before us. Without indulging in a metaphysics which objectifies God, making the Deity one among many beings (even though the Supreme Being) instead of holy being itself, we must recognize and mutually acknowledge the need for extending existential categories into the ontological. Unless we perceive the structures of being in existence which are universal and common to all our cultures, we shall not be able to dialogue on the basis of a shared hermeneutics. How can our symbolic language about God be interpreted for one another and transposed into our own sets of religious symbols if the profound dimensions of reality expressed by the ontological concepts of being, truth, goodness, beauty, intelligence, love, justice, and mercy are not somehow grounding such symbolism! At the same time, we shall not try to celebrate our religious convictions in the language of the literal because we humans shall ever require the poetic power of symbols, which both speak to us in our entirety and also allow us to respond in our total humanness to our God and to our world.

═══ NOTES ═══

1. Frederick Sontag and M. Darrol Bryant, eds., *God: The Contemporary Discussion* (Barrytown, N.Y.: Unification Theological Seminary, 1982), 5–17.

2. Ibid., 15.

3. John Macquarrie, *God-talk: An Examination of the Language and Logic of Theology* (New York: Harper & Row, 1967).

4. Ibid., 168–91.

5. Ibid., 193–94.

6. Ibid., 196.

7. Ibid., 200–201.

8. Aquinas, *Summa Theologiae* 1.3, Timothy McDermott, O. P., trans., in vol. 2: *Existence and Nature of God* (New York: McGraw-Hill, 1964), 19.

9. Cf. ibid., 19–169; Aquinas, *Summa Theologiae* 1.12.12, Herbert McCabe, O. P., trans., in vol. 3: *Knowing and Naming God* (New York: McGraw-Hill, 1964), 41.

10. Macquarrie, 28–29.

11. Aquinas, *Summa Theologiae* 1.13.3, McCabe, 57.

12. Cf. William J. Hill, *Knowing the Unknown God* (New York: Philosophical Library, 1971).

13. Eric Mascall, *Words and Images* (London: Longmans, 1957), 126.

Part Two

NAMES AND CONCEPTS IN DIFFERENT TRADITIONS

Names and Concepts in Different Traditions

4

The Names and Concepts of Deity: Our Languages About Ultimate Reality

SAMUEL A. ADEWALE

In this essay I am going to discuss the concepts of the Deity from the evidence of his names and attributes current among two ethnic groups in Nigeria, namely the Yoruba and the Ibo, whose concepts may be taken as representative throughout Nigeria.

Nigeria is a large country occupied by people of different cultures, languages, and backgrounds. As the cultures are complex so also are the systems of beliefs and religious practices. One may not be surprised to find a many-sided view of the Deity, but the fact that the Deity is variously conceived does not mean that each people had their own God; what it means is that there is the belief in one God, but that God is conceived in different ways by different peoples. However, in the midst of these complexities the Yoruba and the Ibo concepts of the Deity have remained unaffected by foreign and external influences, and this has reflected on their concept of God.

The Yoruba live mainly in Lagos, Ogun, Oyo, Ondo, and parts of Kwara and Bendel states in the southwestern part of Nigeria, while the Ibo are found predominantly in Anambra, Imo, Rivers, and Cross-River states in the southeastern area of Nigeria. Among the two ethnic groups there are names, abundant attributes, proverbs, and sayings which illustrate the concepts of God.

The Yoruba Names of God

Among the Yoruba and other related ethnic groups in Nigeria, names are meaningful and are also significant. They are not just given arbitrarily, but are given to commemorate certain events in the family, or to describe the family lineage of the child, or even to illustrate the natural position or condition of the child at birth. However, every name, whether personal or place, carefully analyzed, will show the intention of the parents or the giver of the name. This idea applies also to the names given to God. Every name of God properly and correctly analyzed reveals what the people actually think, believe, and know about the Deity and the supersensible world.

Principally, the Yoruba have four names for the Supreme Being—the Deity—and these are *Olorun, Oluwa, Eleda* and *Olodumare.* These were the original names of God which were in use before the introduction of Islam and Christianity into the Yoruba land. Dr. S. S. Farrow said:

We find among the Yorubas a belief in a Being called *Olorun,* whose position is unique in several respects, as will be shown. He is regarded by pagans, Mohammedans and Christians alike as the one Supreme Eternal Being, and that this is not due to Mohammedan and Christian influence is evident from the fact that such was the pagan belief before either of the later religions came into the country, and this again is proved by the traditional accounts of creation held by all classes of pagans, particularly those who never come under the influence of foreign religions.[1]

The name *Olorun* in Yoruba is a combination of two words: *Olu* and *Orun. Olu* means "chief" and *Orun* means "heaven." When *Olu* comes into contact with *Orun,* "u" is elided and the two words become *Olorun,* meaning "chief of heaven." The name *Olorun* again may be a combination of *Oni* and *Orun. Oni* means "owner" and *Orun,* as we have seen, means "heaven." In Yoruba grammar when *Oni* comes into contact with *orun, ni* is elided and "l" is substituted and so we have *Olorun* meaning "owner of heaven." The name *Olorun* applied to the Deity means "chief of heaven" or "owner of heaven" or "the chief or supreme being who owns heaven or whose abode is in heaven." This means that God is the Supreme Being or supreme ruler whose abode is in heaven.

It must be noted, however, that heaven in Yoruba is of no definite geographical location. It is everywhere. So when the Deity or the Supreme Being is called "Olorun," he is believed to be everywhere. He is the owner of the heaven above and the earth below. He is the owner of man, animals, birds, plants and trees and in this context the Yoruba regard themselves as his possessions.

The name Olorun shows the Deity as a personal God. It is on the lips of every Yoruba and is commonly used by men, women, boys, and girls.[2] Little children, too, who do not know the connotation of the name use it. The name is used in personal prayers like *Olorun qba mi,* "O God deliver me"; *Olorun sanu mi o,* "O God, have mercy upon me." The name is used as a witness or to prove that one is innocent of an accusation. Thus one frequently hears *Olutun ri mi,* "God sees me," or *Olorun rinu mi,* "God sees my inside that is my heart." The name is used to wish people well, as *Ki Olorun so wa o,* "May God watch over us"; *Ki Olorun so pade o,* "May God wish or permit our meeting again." When a Yoruba receives a blessing, he thanks God and says *Olorun o seun, Olorun mo dupe,* "thank you, God." God is invoked to punish an offender thus: *Olorun yio mu o,* "May God catch you" or *Olorun yio je o niya,* "May God punish you." The name *Olorun* has been in use among the Yoruba from the beginning. I therefore disagree with E. B. Idowu, who said: "The name Olorun is one commonly used in popular language. It appears to have gained its predominating currency in consequence of Christian and Moslem impact upon Yoruba thought: it is the name used mostly in evangelistic work and in literature."[3] Dr. S. S. Farrow, who spent several years in Yoruba land and acquired the working knowledge of the language, was also opposed to this idea, as I have quoted above.[4]

The Yoruba are very anthropomorphic about their concept of God. He is a potent being and can be invoked to act like human beings. Olorun causes rain to fall and sun to shine. He makes land fertile and gives food to all his creatures. He brings about light and darkness and, as the owner of the world, he continues to maintain it. He is very active in the world. This is why he is invoked every time and everywhere. For this reason I do not agree with A. B. Ellis who, when writing about Olorun, said: "Since he is too lazy or too indifferent to exercise any control over earthly affairs, man on his side does not waste time in endeavoring to propitiate him, but reserves his worship and sacrifice for more active agents."[5]

This view of Ellis's was a product of ignorance and prejudice. Ignorance because he did not understand the Yoruba tradition. The Yoruba do not approach their rulers directly because they are supreme and majestic in their positions as human rulers. The people will approach them or send gifts to them through their (rulers') attendants. In the religious situation Olorun, "the Supreme Being," is supreme and majestic—too supreme to be approached directly. And since there are intermediaries between humans and him, humans approach him through the intermediaries. All offerings and sacrifices are sent to him through the intermediaries, but the acceptance of the offerings and answers to man's requests are his exclusive prerogative. Ellis's view was also a product of prejudice because Ellis, like others, would not want to believe that Africans could have religion or knowledge of God like the Western people. Emil Ludwig's contention about African ideas of God is an illustration of this prejudicial notion. Ludwig said: "How can the untutored Africans conceive God? . . . How can this be? Deity is a philosophical concept which savages are incapable of framing."[6] Objective analyses of the names and attributes of God show clearly that Africans have knowledge of God.

The Yoruba see Olorun as a present help in time of need, and as one who is always present with man in his house, at his place of work, on his journey, and in his play. They feel his presence with them and so they do not hesitate to invoke him as an intimate father, friend, or helper. Olorun is not merely a power but is also a person. Hence the use of anthropomorphic terms. He is neither a remote God nor a withdrawn God. Here again Ellis was wrong when he said: "Olorun is the sky god of the Yoruba; that is, he is deified firmament, or personal sky. . . . He is merely a nature god, the personality divine sky, and he only controls phenomena connected in the native mind with the roof of the world."[7]

Another Yoruba name of God which illustrates what they believe about him is *Oluwa*. Like Olorun, Oluwa is a combination of two words: *Olu* and *awa*. *Olu*, as we have seen above, means "chief" and *awa* is a possessive pronoun meaning "our." When *Olu* comes into contact with *awa*, the vowel "a" of *awa* is elided, and so we have Olu-wa, meaning "our chief," the chief or the Supreme Being who owns us. In one word it means "our Lord" or simply "Lord." So when the Yoruba call the Deity "Oluwa" they ascribe to him the ownership of the whole universe. Several Yoruba traditional rulers have the title of *olu* (chief, ruler, Lord), which in other towns is the same as *oba* (king). The chief of Ibadan, the capitol of the state of Oyo, is Olu'badan; the supreme chief of Ilaro town in the state of Ogun is Olu-Ilaro; while the chief of Iwo, a town in the state of Oyo, is called Olu-Iwo or Oluwo. These chiefs are kings in their capacities. Oluwa is the Lord with absolute authority. In his capacity as the Lord he has power to build and to destroy, to save and to kill, to reward and to punish. Oluwa is the supreme chief; he is the ruler or king with unlimited power. He is the head of the theocratic government of the universe with the divinities as his ministers.[8] He is in the world, active and acting.

The name Oluwa is as frequently used as Olorun, and the expressions connected with it illustrate the belief of the Yoruba in the Deity. The name is used in popular language, ejaculatory prayers, and in proverbs. Sometimes Oluwa and Olorun are used interchangeably and sometimes both together as *Oluwa Olorun mi, sanu mi,* "My Lord God have mercy upon me." When the Yoruba are going to bed at night they say *Ki Oluwa ki oji wa 're o,* "May the Lord wake us up well," or *Ki Oluwa ki o so wa o,* "May the Lord watch over us." When they are parting, the host says to the guest *mo fi Oluwa sin o o,* "I wish the Lord to go with you." The host may say, *"Ki Oluwa ki ofe ipade o,* "May the Lord keep us and make our meeting again possible." The Lord can be invoked as a witness to a statement if it is doubted. Thus, it is said *Oluwa ngbo,* "the Lord hears" or *Oluwa ri mi,* "the Lord sees me." The Yoruba believe that it is the Supreme Being that makes things possible, so when they want to embark on a project they say *Bi Oluwa ba fe,* "if the Lord wills it" or *Bi o ba se ife Oluwa,* "if it is the wish of the Lord." The frequent use of the name has made the Deity a household property of the Yoruba—not as a tool, but as a familiar master.

The name Oluwa also appears to show the Deity as a person. He has life, consciousness, and knowledge. He is always active and acting in the world.[9] Oluwa is a moral Deity who rewards good deeds and punishes evil deeds.

The third name of the Deity is *Olodumare,* which simply means "almighty." Like the first two names, the name Olodumare is a compound word of three syllables, namely *oni-odu-mare.* In Yoruba *Oni* means "owner," as we have seen before, *Odu* means "chief," "supreme," "greatest," "largest"; and *Odu* means "chapter" in the corpus of Ifa recitals, or "chief head" or "scepter."[10] The meaning of *Odu* depends on the tone marks put upon its vowels. When *Oni* comes into contact with *Odu, ni,* as usual, is elided and "l" substituted, as in the case of Olorun, so we have Olodu "the biggest owner" or "the chief owner of scepter."

The third syllable of the name, *mare,* is of controversial meaning. J. O. Lucas gave the meaning of the word as *maa re* ("I shall go" or "I must go").[11] In this context Olodumare means "the chief or the supreme chief to whom I must go or return" or "the chief owner of scepter of authority to whom I shall go," that is, after death.

E. B. Idowu has suggested several meanings for the word *mare,* but only one of the suggestions is relevant for our purpose. According to this suggestion the word *mare* means "do not go or do not proceed." The phrase may also be a descriptive adjective meaning "that does not go," "that does not move or wander," "that remains," "that continues."[12] In this context Olodumare means "the chief or supreme being who possesses the scepter of authority and does not move" or "the owner of authority who remains unchanged." Whichever meaning we accept, Lucas's or Idowu's, the name is controversial and pregnant with meaning. What is certain about it is that it connotes the almightiness of God. It is a name that embodies the meanings of other names of the Deity and the functions connected with them.

Olodumare is the name that shows the absolute supremacy of the Deity, and for this reason it is rarely used in common language. Other names of the Deity are always used; and whenever Olodumare is mentioned, some attributes follow to show who or what he is or what he can do. For instance, the Yoruba say *Olodumare Oba ti a kikiki ti a ko le ki tan, Olodumare* (the king with endless or innumerable attributes); *Olodumare Oba Adake dajo, Olodumare* (the king who executes judgment in silence); *Olodumare Oba Asore kari aye, Olodumare* (the king whose mercy is spread all over the universe).[13]

Olodumare is a name that shows the nature and essence of the Deity. It connotes love, mercy, power and authority of the Deity. It also shows him as a friend, father, and helper. Idowu said: "The name Olodumare has always carried with it the idea of one with Whom man may enter into covenant or communion in any place and at any time, one who is supreme, superlatively great, incomparable and unsurpassable in majesty, excellent in attributes, stable, unchanging, constant, reliable."[14]

The fourth in the series of the names of the Supreme Being—the Deity—among the Yoruba which is descriptive of his nature and being is *Eleda*. The name Eleda simply means "creator," but by breaking the word into its component parts, *Oni-Eda*, it means "owner of creation or creatures." *Oni* in Yoruba means "owner" and *Eda* means "creation" or "creatures." In Yoruba grammar, when *oni* comes into contact with the vowel "e" or *eda*, an elision of *Oni* takes place and "El" is substituted. So we have "El" + *eda* becoming *Eleda*.[15] *Eleda*, "owner of creation or creatures," or simply "creator," a name that is used in common language by individuals and groups.

The Deity, in his capacity as Eleda, is credited with the creation of heaven and earth. He is *Eleda orun on aye*, "the Creator of heaven and earth." He created all things in heaven and on earth. If a Yoruba man or woman is asked, "Who made you?" he or she will have no problem to say "God made me." If the same question is asked in respect of other objects, the answer will also be "God made them." The name Eleda is constantly used in soliloquy, especially when the Yorubas find themselves in a dilemma. In such a case the Deity is referred to as a personal God, and the Yoruba says in a distressed tone *Eleda mi 'jowo sanu mi,* "O my Creator, please, have mercy upon me" or *Eleda mi jowo qba mi,* "O my Creator please deliver me." Sometimes he or she beseeches the Creator not to forget him or her, and talks to him in a personal way saying, *Eleda mi ma ma gbagbe mi,* "O, my Creator, please do not forget me." In a new venture the Yoruba solicits the help of his Creator and says *Eleda mi ma je ki nte,* "May my Creator let me not suffer ridicule or ignominy," or for somebody else as *Eleda re ko ni je ki ote,* "May your Creator let you not suffer ridicule or ignominy." When a Yoruba receives a blessing or achieves a success in his project, he or she attributes the success to the Creator and thanks him in the following words: *Eleda mi o seun,* "My Creator, thank you." When life is not well with somebody the Yoruba may see as one of the causes of the misfortune an offense against the person's Creator. In that case the person consults the diviners in order to know the measure for the reparation of the damaged relationship. This shows that the Creator can be offended and appeased.

The Yoruba invoke the Creator not only in prayers and intercessions but also in songs. They compose original songs, lyrics and choruses to pour out their minds to the Deity. These direct and personal addresses and requests prove Talbot's assertion about the relationship between the Yoruba and *Olorun* to be wrong. Talbot said: "He is deemed to be far away and to take little interest in mankind; direct appeal is only made to him as a last resource. As a rule, all prayers and sacrifices are offered to the Orisha, and if necessary, through these mediators, to the Awlawrun."[16]

The Yoruba offer their prayers and intercessions directly to Olorun as the need arises, without going through any intermediary. They offer sacrifices through intermediaries because the intermediaries are messengers of the Supreme Being and, just as they do not approach their rulers directly, they consider it a dishonor to approach the Supreme Being directly. This assertion was also made by Lucas when he said:

The relegation of the worship of Olorun to the background does not lead to an entire ignorance of him as the Supreme Deity. Although he is regarded as too holy and exalted to be approached directly with sacrifices . . . yet He is regarded as taking cognizance of, and active interest in, the affairs of men when necessary. He is not an absentee God, Who, after creating the world refused to be bothered with its affairs and safeguarded Himself by locking Himself up behind the metal sheet of the clouds. . . . But short prayers are often offered to Him, and these show the existence of a belief in His readiness to help in times of urgent necessity or dire calamity, a belief in His activity in the world, and a recognition of gratitude to Him as a special duty incumbent upon man. . . .[17]

The Yoruba always feel the presence of the Deity and believe in his power to save, deliver, protect, and help. So they call on him very often in their places of work, on their journeys, in their homes, in time of joy, in time of sorrow, and in their devotions. They also believe that the Creator can be provoked, can punish, can hinder and can be appeased. So they tend to keep his injunctions in order to avoid his wrath.

All the names of the Deity highlighted above can be used by anybody without any prerequisite qualifications. We have seen their meanings overlap; and, in addition to the common function, each name has specific duty attached to the meaning. They all reveal the Deity as being actively present in the world and as being a personal God. Hence the positive attitude of the Yoruba toward him.

Ibo Names of God

In my brief introduction I stated that each people have their own concept of the Deity and that to some extent the concepts overlap. In this part of the essay I want to examine what the Ibo think, believe, and know about the Deity from the evidence of the names given to him.

While the Yoruba have four principal names of God, the Ibo have two, namely, *Chukwu* and *Chineke*.[18] These two names show what they really know about him. The names are employed in conversations, and personal and ritual prayers. They are employed in order to express anger and disgust.

Like the Yoruba Olodumare, Chukwu is pregnant with meaning. It is an embodiment of all that the Deity is. It is a compound name of two component parts: *Chi* and *Ukwu*. *Chi* means "source," "origin," "pool," and *Ukwu* means "great." The Ibo grammar behaves like the Yoruba grammar in certain ways. When two words are brought into contact with each other to form a compound word, elision generally takes place. So when *Chi* comes into contact with *Ukwu*, the "i" of Chi is elided, giving way to the "u" of Ukwu, so that we have Ch-Ukwu written in one word as Chukwu, meaning "great source," "great origin," "great pool." When it is applied to the Deity it means "the great source of being" or "the great origin of being" or "the great pool from which everything originates." He is the Supreme *Chi* (God).

By this name the Ibo believe that everything and every event in the world has its origins in the Deity. Nothing comes into being by chance and nothing happens by chance. A man does not die or experience sickness or misfortune by fortuity; the wind does not blow nor the rain fall nor the lightning flash by chance. A man does not acquire wealth by his own efforts, and poverty is not to be seen as the fault of the poor. Chukwu is the great cause of everything.[19] He is to be seen in every act, through the medium of one of his agents. All the forces of the world are directed by him.

The Ibo always invoke Chukwu like a personal friend. They even invite him to share kolanuts with them during ritual ceremonies. Thus they say, *Chukwu ta oji,* meaning "Chukwu, come and eat kola."

Chukwu has many attributes[20] and many Ibo personal names derive from his name: all these indicate what Chukwu is, what he has done, what he can do and what he is doing. *Chukwuemeka* means "God has done marvelous, great is his name;" *Nwachukwu* means "Son of Chukwu 'God'," while *Okechukwu* means "God's gift." *Oke-Chukwu* again means "the strength of God." What the Ibo understand by Oke-Chukwu is that man's well-being depends on the power of God. Other personal names deriving from Chukwu include *Aja-Chukwu,* meaning "God's sacrifice" or "God's gift"; *Chukura* meaning "God or Supreme Chi leaves or spares." This means it is Chukwu (God/Supreme Chi) who spares this child. *Chukudi* means "God (Chukwu) exists."

The second Ibo name of the Deity is *Chineke,* and it is self-explanatory. It is a descriptive name like the Yoruba *Eleda*. It is a combination of three syllables, *Chi, na* and *eke*.[21] *Chi* as we have seen above is the "source of being." Parrinder described it as "soul."[22] The second syllable *na* means "who" or "is" and the third syllable *eke* means "create." When the three words are put together we have Chi-na-eke, but when *na* comes into contact with *eke,* elision of one of the two vowels takes place. In this case the vowel "a" of *na* is elided, and we have *neke*. When *Chi* joins *neke* we have Chineke, meaning "Chi who created," "the being or spirit who created," or simply "creator," and God is believed to be the Creator; so Chineke is the Supreme Being, the Deity or God.

The concept of God as the Creator is well-defined and well-emphasized among the Ibo. As the Yoruba call Olorun very often, so the Ibo, too, call Chineke. The name is a household word among the Ibo, who use it in conversations, as a witness to statements, in a curse to an offender and in personal prayers. The frequent use of the name is a strong evidence of belief in him as a personal God and as a close friend or father. He is near and around, guarding and guiding his people. Talbot says ". . . he takes an interest in mankind, and it is upon him, together with the personal Chi, that the length of a man's life depends."[23]

Several expressions, proverbs, and names deriving from or connecting with Chineke are always on the lips of the Ibo. The Ibo thank Chineke for all blessings of food, fertility, rain at the right time, children, health, and deliverance from danger. Talbot again says: "Each morning among most Ika, as with many other Ibo, every man or woman, on rising, raises his hands to heaven, rubs them together and says 'God, I thank you for long life,' and if a child has been born, 'I thank you for my child,' etc.—and prays for help for the day."[24]

The root or key word of both Chukwu and Chineke is Chi (God). It precedes several words and sometimes it is added as suffix to some words or names or expressions. Thus the Ibo say, *Chi Kpuru nnunu nyere ya oche na, ukwu ya,* "the God who created the bird provided a seat for it with its feet." They say, *Chi nyere nwata ja awon n'enye ya mbazu oji eqwu ya,* "God provides us with sufficient grace with which we can overcome the problems and trials of this world." Personal names having *Chi* as prefix or suffix include *Chinyere,* meaning "God gave," that is, "given by God"; *Chibuzor,* meaning "God is the way, or road, or path"; *Chijioke,* meaning "God holds his man's share or portion"; and *Onyechi,* meaning "the divine essence is a personal God."

The Ibo believe that success or failure in life is not the result of a person's own efforts or indolence. If one is great it is one's Chi that has made one that way, and if anyone is wretched, the traditional Ibo would not blame the individual for the wretched-ness. This belief finds expression in the saying: *Omere ma chi ekweghi o nye nta atala ya* meaning "if one strives to survive but his God does not allow his survival, let no one blame him." The cordial relation-ship with and personal attitude toward the Deity among the Ibo show that he is in close contact, near, and living. I do not agree with Talbot when he said: "Chi lives far away in the depths of the sky, but is not quite so distant as among the Yoruba."[25] What Talbot means by "living far away in the depths of the sky" and "not quite so distant as among the Yoruba" is not clear. The attributes of the Deity, as we shall see in the next section, also prove the assertion of Talbot wrong. Recent and personal investigations have shown that such ideas as "distant or high God" or "withdrawn God" are prejudicial, obnoxious and inappropriate. To Africans, God is gen-erally not far away. Dr. Lucas said: "The Olorun of the Yorubas is not 'the deified firmament' or 'merely a nature god' or 'a sky-god' . . ."[26]

Attributes

In addition to names, there are attributes of God which are descrip-tive of his nature, being, and essence. Indeed, these attributes throw light on the people's understanding and knowledge of him as a living reality, active and continuously operating in the universe. We shall now look at some of the attributes.

God is described as King. Several Yoruba words and expressions show God as king, with attributes in the superlative degree. The Yoruba word for king is *Oba* and the Ibo word for it is *Eze*. In the traditional society the king is the supreme ruler of the people. The world is believed to be God's world and he is seen as the king of the theocratic government of the world, with heavenly ministers as his subjects. So this concept is based upon the structure in the society. The Yoruba call him *Oba Orun* "heavenly king" or "king in heaven," while the Ibo call him *Eze di n'elu* or *Eze echi* or *Eze enigwe,* meaning "heavenly king." Almost every attribute of the Deity among the Yoruba, as we shall see, carries the word *oba,* "king," with it.

In his capacity as the king, the Deity is the supreme ruler of the universe, and the stability and smooth running of the government is his main preoccupation. It is believed that the earthly kings and chiefs are put in authority by him and in this context the Yoruba describe him as *Oba orun ti o nfi Oba aye je* "the heavenly king who installs or enthrones the earthly king." Whenever the Yoruba see or hear any event that is exciting or alarming, they acknowledge the Deity as a wonderful king and pay royal tribute to him by saying *Kabiyesi Olodumare* "Your majesty, O Lord." He is the king with absolute power and authority; the heavenly bodies and other beings take directives from him.

God is Judge. The Supreme Deity is described as a judge with absolute authority. He is the just judge of the final court of appeal. Against his judgment there is no appeal, and in his court no solicitor or counsel is required, because he is a righteous judge. He will never pervert justice, and his judgment takes place not only after death but here on earth, before death. Thus, when a Yoruba feels cheated or wronged, he or she leaves the judgment to God and says *Olorun yio se 'dajo o,* "God will judge"; and whenever a wicked person suffers, the Yoruba say *Olorun l'o muu,* "it is God who has punished him," and whenever a Yoruba cannot revenge a wrongdoing he or she leaves the cheat in the hands of God for judgment.

In his capacity as the great judge, the Supreme Deity is described as *Oba Adakedajo* "a king who judges in silence."[27] He does not make any proclamation about his judgment. The judgment is seen in the sufferings or misfortunes of wicked or mischievous persons. The concept of judgment is seen as a phenomenon that starts from this world, while the final judgment is postponed till after "death." Each person goes immediately after his death to the judgment hall to receive judgment according to his deeds on earth. But the African concept or doctrine of judgment differs from that of either Christians or Muslims in that it is not delayed till a remote time in post-modern history. The Yoruba or the Ibo do not believe that God punishes the righteous; rather than punishing, he rewards them, and when a righteous person suffers, the Yoruba have no difficulty in finding a solution to this problem. God is always good. The suffering or misfortune of the righteous person caused by evil forces is attributed to the wickedness of his parents or grandparents. This doctrine of corporate living and corporate sharing is very strong in African traditional religion. Thus the Yoruba say *Aqba t'okunle t'o qb'ebu ika b'o pe titi omo re y'o je nibe,* "An elderly person who kneels down and plants the yam set of wickedness, in the distant future his children will eat of it." The goodness of God also finds expression in the saying *Olorun ko se 'bi,* "God never does evil."

Again, the Yoruba do not see every suffering or misfortune of a righteous person as punishment of God to destroy the person, that is, not necessarily as a punishment for evil, but as a means of helping the person. Thus they see illness which prevents a person from going on a proposed journey as a prevention from a more serious misfortune. This belief finds an expression in the saying *Bi Olorun ba nse rere a wipe on nse 'bi,* "When God is doing good we say he is doing evil."

God is Unique. God is above all things in heaven and on earth. He has no companions and no associates. There is no other being like him. Among the Yoruba and the Iba and in Nigeria generally, God is not represented with graven images or moulded objects. There is nothing to compare or to liken him to. The Yoruba, in praising him, call him as *Oba ti ko l'egbe, Oba ti ko l'afi jo, Oba ni'kansoso,* "a king who has no companion, a king who has no likeness, the only one king." He cannot be compared in greatness, in essence, in nature, and in function with any other object. Of him Lucas said: "Over and above all the other deities classified above and excelling them in power, honor and majesty is the Supreme Deity known as Olorun, a Being of unique character possessing attributes far too noble, far too abstract and refined to have originated from the thought of a primitive people.[28] All the attributes of the Supreme Deity are in the superlative degree and every one of the attributes reflects him as a unique Deity. J. S. Mbiti said, "Many of the attributes of God . . . give him a high, indeed, a unique status, so that he is pre-eminent in all things."[29]

God is Immortal. It is believed that God cannot die. All other things will perish because they were made with perishable materials. Only God will remain forever. In his capacity as immortal Deity, the Yoruba describe him as *Oyigiyigi Oba Aiku* "Immovable, the undying king." The Ibo say "if God were to die, he should have died, but because he is immortal he lives till now." The Yoruba also describe him as *Arugbo ojo jojo, Alagaba igbani* "the very old man, the elder of those old days." It is believed that God is never ill, no man can harm him, and no evil can befall him. He is *Olodumare eniti apa omo araye koko 'Olodumare,* "one who cannot be overcome by all the forces of evil man." It is again said, *Ofere gege, a ki igbo'ku Olodumare, ofere gege* "No, never, we do not hear the death of Olodumare, no, never."

God is Creator. Generally, all the names of the supreme Deity show him as creator God. He created everything and he continues to create and to maintain. The Ibo call him *Eze kere enugwe n'ala* "the king who created heaven and earth." The Yoruba name Eleda, "Creator," connotes creation, and his creative work continues in sending rain to make the land fertile, the sun to make the fruits ripe, and food to sustain living beings. He maintains the universe through a retinue of intermediaries. He created according to his prerogative. The albinos, the hunchbacks, and the dwarfs are special marks of his prerogatives and sometimes of his displeasure. This kind of creation is never ridiculed but it is regarded as *Ise Olodumare* "the work of the Deity," which God created either by himself, or through the instrumentality of lesser gods, who took instructions from him. Even when other gods are connected with creation, the supreme Deity is believed to be the creator of everything.[30] Everything owes its existence to him. Thus, the Ibo call him *Onye nwe Uwu* "the owner of the world." As the creator and owner of the world, everything depends upon him for sustenance.

God is All-Powerful. The almightiness and all-powerfulness of God is perfectly contained in the names Olodumare and Chukwu. God is great and great in his work. He is able to do everything and to do it perfectly. His works are wonderful and mysterious. In his position as the all-powerful God, the Yoruba described him as *Oba Asekan ma ku,* "the king who does everything to perfection," or "the king who leaves no stone unturned." Every event, whether good or bad has its basis in God, as the great cause of everything. Although African theology shows that God is good and does not do evil, as seen in the Yoruba saying *Olorun ko s'ebi* "God does not do evil," all agents of action are set in motion on earth as his instruments, and nothing happens without his knowledge or permission. This concept is illustrated by the saying *Bi Olorun ko pani, Oba kopani* "If God does not kill, the king cannot kill." This implies that it is when God allows something that human beings can do it. Thus Idowu said of Olodumare:

He is able to do all things; He is the Enabler of all who achieve any ends. Things are possible only when and because they are ordered by him; they are impossible when he does not permit them or give his aid. This is what we mean when we say *A-dun-se bi ohun ti Olodumare se, a-soro'se bi ohun ti Olorun ko lowo si* "Easy to do as that which Olodumare performs; difficult to do as that which Olorun enables not. . . ."[31]

This includes both the good and the evil things.

With God, it is believed nothing is impossible. He is *Olorun Alaqbara* "God the powerful." The Ibo name *Mgbeodichimma* is a call to leave everything for God whenever humans try and fail. His works are so wonderful, so mysterious, and so mighty that no human ever challenges him. The Yoruba offer thanks to God for any punishment believed to be inflicted by him.

God is All-Knowing. The belief that God sees and knows everything is very strong among both the Yoruba and the Ibo. God sees in the darkness and knows the secrets of the human heart. When the Yoruba want to prove innocence of a crime or an allegation, they say *Olotun rinu mi,* "God sees my inside," "God sees my heart." Or they say *Ohun ti o pamo oju Olorun lo to* "what is hidden, it is God who knows it." This statement attributes knowledge of everything, including what lies in the depths below, to God. No one except God alone knows and sees the heart of the wicked. All men look alike, and to this end the Yoruba say *Olorun l'orikun ase ka, on na lo rikun asooto,* "It is God who sees the heart of the wicked and it is he too who sees the heart of the righteous." The Yoruba have several choruses to show their belief in the power of God to know everything. One such chorus is:

A, onwo o o: It is looking at you,
Oju Oluwa: The Eye of the Lord,
A, o nwo o o: It is looking at you.

God is also described as *Oba Arinu r'ode Olumo okan* "the king who sees the inside, the knower of the secret of the heart." He sees the evil that a person plans or does in secret, and to this the Yoruba say *A molun jale bi oba aye ko ri o, Oba orun nwo o,* "You who steal in darkness, if the earthly king does not see you, the heavenly king is looking at you." Again, to show the belief that God knows everything and sees in darkness, it is said *O yido bori o ta 'fa s'oke, O l'enikan ori o, Oba Oluwa nwo o pelu ise re,* "You cover yourself with mortar and you shoot an arrow upwards saying nobody sees you, Lord the king is looking at you with your work." All these sayings about the knowledge of everything serve to discourage evil in the society and to encourage good deeds.

God is Everywhere (Omnipresent). The belief that the supreme Deity is everywhere finds expressions in sayings, actions, and proverbs among the Yoruba and the Ibo. The Yoruba call the supreme Deity *Oba Atererekari aye* "the king who is spread all over the world." In his capacity as One who is present everywhere in the world the Ibo describe him as *Eze Uwa nine* "the king of the whole world," or *Onye nwe Uwa,* "the owner of the world." He is also *Ozuru mba onu* "One who covers everywhere." The Yoruba, by virtue of God's being everywhere, believe that he can be worshipped anywhere without assigning a particular shrine to him. Hence, they call him *Oba ti ko ni ojubo,* "the king who has no shrine." Because God can be worshipped anywhere, there are no temples built to him, as this would make nonsense of the whole theology, and would be a contradiction of it. It would also mean the confinement of the king of the whole universe to a small place. The absence of temples of the Deity has made some white investigators of African traditional religion conclude that the Deity is not worshipped at all in some parts of Africa.[32]

God is Transcendent. The names and attributes of the Deity connote transcendence. He transcends everything. His transcendence does not mean remoteness or being removed from the world, but it is in terms of honor, majesty, supremacy, power, love and mercy. As the Creator, the judge, the king, and preserver of the whole world he must possess attributes that excell those of other things, including human beings, animals, and gods. He is unique. He is the giver of wisdom, knowledge and intellect. He is *Oba orun ti o nfi oba aye je,* "the heavenly king that enthrones the earthly king." He surpasses everything.

God is Merciful. Although African theology shows that God can be provoked, he is merciful. He is the dear father of his children and he loves them. He helps those in trouble and provides for the needy ones. His mercy toward the world and all his creatures is infinite. He provides for the birds of the sky, the fishes in the seas, and the ants that crawl on the ground. He maintains the world by sending rain, sun, and the wind that blows at the right time. His hands are hands of mercy. He is described as *Olowo gbogboro ti o nyo omo re l'ofin,* "One with long arms of mercy to rescue his children from the pit." Again the Deity is seen as the helper of the helpless, and in this regard the Yoruba say *Malu ti ko ni 'ru Olorun l'onle esinsin fun u,* "A cow without tail, it is God that drives away flies for it." The Ibo describe the Deity as *Enye-maka o nye ogbenye,* "the helper of the poor." He is also described as *Chineke Onye ebere,* "God of mercy." The Yoruba see him as *Oba ti o ngba alailara,* "the king who delivers those who have no relations." He is *Ogbagba ti igba aradugbo,* "the defender," *Olupese,* "the provider" and *Oluranlowo alaini,* "the helper of the needy." The Yoruba believe that God alone can give children, so they say *Olorun ni 'se omo,* "it is God who makes children." The Ibo describe him as *Aka n'enye Omumu,* "the hand that gives children," *Aka n'enye aku,* "the hand that gives wealth."

The supreme Deity can be propitiated with sacrifice and can be invoked in times of crises and calamities for succor and help. The Yoruba say *Olorun sanu mu o,* "O God, have mercy upon me," or *Olorum qba mi o,* "O my God, please deliver me." In time of trouble, and in time of joy after a blessing has been received, they give thanks to God and say *Olorun o seun,* "thank you, God," or *Olorun mi mo dupe,* "I thank you, O my God." *O Chukwu emeka!* among the Ibo is an exclamation of joy and it means that God should be praised for his mercy. *Chukwu nwe ndu onye na efu offia* means "God protects his lost dear ones," while *Nke Chukwu nyelu moduka ife nine* means "God's gift supersedes man's." Because people women believe in the steadfast love of God, they turn to him always for help.

God is Incomprehensible. The incomprehensibility of the works of God is illustrated by the positive attitude of the Yoruba and the Ibo toward him. Generally, his existence is not doubted, as we have seen in the discussions on the names given to him. He is wonderful and mysterious, and the way he operates is beyond the understanding of humans. Whenever an event happens which Africans cannot explain, they simply attribute the cause to God. The Yoruba believe that "the work of God is unsearchable," *awanaridi nise Olodumare.* In this context the Ibo describe him as *Chineke di ebuke* "the wonderful and mysterious God." His attributes are innumerable because he is wonderful. He is *Oba ti a kikiki ti a ko le ki tan,* "the king whose attributes or praise names are inexhaustible." The Africans regard the risings and settings of the sun and the moon, the blowing of the wind, the falling of the rain, the growing of crops, and bearing of fruits by crops as proofs of his wonderfulness. The Yoruba or the Ibo or Africans in general will get stuck if they are confronted with questions about how these phenomena take place. The answer will be "They are works of God." Then the Yoruba will say, "*'eniti o ba nwadi ise Olodumare yio sonu*" ("He who wants to know the secret of the work of the Supreme God will get lost)".

The names and attributes of the Deity that we have discussed in this essay significantly suggest that the ideas about God were not introduced to the Yoruba and the Ibo from outside, and suggest that the names were not foreign to them. Dr. Farrow said, "The Yorubas have a clear conception of the one Supreme Deity."[33] Dr. Lucas, who was himself a Yoruba and was in close contact with the religious thought of his people, strongly and firmly supports Dr. Farrow's assertion.[34]

There are many more attributes which are descriptive of the nature of the Deity, but because of the limited scope of this essay I have confined myself to the very important ones, and do believe that these are adequate proofs of the concepts of the Deity among the people. However, no nation in the world possesses perfect knowledge of God, and if the Yoruba and the Ibo have imperfect or partial knowledge of him, it is due to his incomprehensible nature and, like other nations, they are not to be condemned for it.

NOTES

1. Stephen S. Farrow, *Faith, Fancies, and Fetish of Yoruba Paganism* (London: S.P.C.K., 1926), 24. See also Geoffrey Parrinder, *West African Religion* (London: The Epworth Press, 1949), 12.

2. E. B. Idowu, *Olodumare: God in Yoruba Belief* (London: n. p., 1962), 37.

3. Ibid., 37.

4. Farrow, 24.

5. A. B. Ellis, *The Yoruba-Speaking Peoples of the Slave Coast of Africa* (London, 1894), 36f.

6. *African Ideas of God,* ed. E. W. Smith (London: Edinburgh House, 1950), 1.

7. Ellis, 36.

8. Idowu, 40.

9. We will say more about *Oluwa* under attributes.

10. See also Idowu, 34–36.

11. J. O. Lucas, *The Religion of the Yorubas* (Lagos: C.M.S. Bookshop, 1948), 41.

12. Idowu, 36.

13. Ibid.

14. Ibid.

15. Ayo Bamgbose, *A Grammar of Yoruba* (Cambridge: Cambridge University Press, 1966), 160f.

16. Percy A. Talbot, *The Peoples of Southern Nigeria,* vol. 2 (London: Frank Cass Co., 1969).

17. Lucas, 45.

18. Parrinder, 21–22.

19. Ibid., 21.

20. These will be discussed under the section on attributes.

21. Percy Talbot, *The Peoples of Southern Nigeria,* vol. 2 (London: Clarke, Doble & Brendon, 1926), 40.

22. Parrinder, 21. When *Chi* is described as soul, it indicates the essence of being, that which makes man a living being.

23. Talbot, 40.

24. Ibid.

25. Ibid.

26. Lucas, 35.

27. Idowu, 42.

28. Lucas, 34.

29. Parrinder, 20.

30. Idowu, 39; Parrinder, 20.

31. Idowu, 41.

32. Parrinder, 19.

33. Farrow, 29.

34. Lucas, 35.

5

The Name and Concepts of God Among the Buem and the Akan of Ghana

JOHN K. ANSAH

I have chosen the topic "The Names and Concepts of God Among the Buem and the Akan of Ghana" for this reason: Coming from as far away as Ghana in (West) Africa, I thought it would be of interest to discuss with you what the African, in the person of the Ghanaian, knows about a Supreme Deity. This, I felt, would minimize the danger of my boring the reader with familiar material if I should talk about Western people.

The People of Buem- and Akan-land

Who are the Buem and the Akan whose religious mind this essay explores? Administratively, the Buem district embraces many small minority groups of people. But in this essay I take the Buem to be the *Lelemi* speaking people who live in an area northeast of the Volta region of Ghana. Tradition shows that the Lelemi speaking people are the original settlers of the Buem area. They speak their own language, which is called *Lelemi* or *Lefana*. As the people who speak the Lelemi or Lefana language are also called *Balemi* or *Bafana,* I shall simply refer to them all as the Buem.

The Akan are the people who speak the Twi language of Ghana with variations in dialect. They occupy most of the central and southern belts of Ghana. Linguistically, they are the largest single ethnic group in the country.

The various traditions about the origin of the Buem substantially agree that the Buem are of Akan origin, indeed, that they are Akan. Migration brought them to the area they now occupy. This apparently explains the fact that the Buem have mostly Akan names, a pattern of chieftaincy which is the same as that of the Akan of Ashanti tribe, and almost all their practices are Akan.[1]

As noted above, the Buem speak their own language. So do the

Akan. Therefore a lot of indigenous religious ideas can be discovered in their languages. However, since the two peoples are from the same stock and have identical practices, it is to be expected that their religious ideas are basically the same. For this reason, what is said of the religious thinking of one applies for the most part to the other. It also explains why I concern myself not with the Buem or the Akan alone, but with both.

No clear-cut distinction between the names and concepts will be made. The God-names themselves portray the ideas the Buem and the Akan have of God.

Belief in God

A brief outline of the religions in Ghana is telling of the fact that "Christian belief was already present in Ghanaian traditional religion with its sense of an almighty God over all other gods and things."[2]

Christian missionary work started in the Gold Coast, now Ghana, when the Portuguese missionaries first landed on the shores of the Gold Coast and erected a cross at a coastal village called Shama in 1471.[3] Thus before Christianity came to Ghana over five hundred years ago, the Buem and the Akan knew and believed in God. They knew that there exists a great God, a Supreme Being unequalled in power by any other god. Their knowledge of him and belief in him could only spring independently out of their reflection on nature—reflection on the things around them. The conception of the Akan that a child simply grows up to know God is an allusion to the acquisition of knowledge of God and belief in him in this way. An Akan proverb aptly expresses this conception: *Obi nkyere abofra Nyame*, "Nobody shows God to a child." And how do children come to know God if God is not shown to them, or if they are not taught about God? The child can know him only from surrounding nature. It may be concluded too that this means the Buem and the Akan consider the knowledge of God to be inborn in humans. Even so, that knowledge must still be actualized by observing nature.

The Buem or the Akan have a philosophical reason for thinking that nature reveals God and as such they can derive some knowledge of God from it. They see that there are causes and effects, things that cause others to be, and things that are caused to be. They believe that here cause and the effect cannot be totally unlike, but that there must be a similarity between them. A cause must give something of its own riches, it must share something of what it has to the effect. In short, a cause must produce something similar to itself. The Buem or the Akan does not put it so philosophically, but they say it all the same in one proverb. The Buem says: *Kedu kala wo akwan*—"An antelope does not beget a bush pig." Changing the animals, the Akan has it that: "A crab does not beget a bird." The other side of this metaphysical principle proverbially stated is that a crab begets a crab. A human being begets a human being. From a living thing a living thing comes. A cause, therefore, is always similar to its effect. An artist leaves something (signs) of his genius on all his paintings. This is why the work of one artist is distinguishable from the work of another artist, for example, the paintings of the Spanish artist Bartolome Esteban Murillo from those of the Italian artist Michelangelo Buonarroti. Consequently, a quality which is found in an effect must be found in the cause. If, therefore, God created all things and us human beings, we must be in some way like him, for an effect is always in some way similar to its cause. We must bear his imprints; we must have his image.[4]

Before contact with Christianity, the Buem or the Akan had seen nature to possess some qualities. To them, nature is in some way similar to God, who made it. It reflects God to some extent. In this way they see the phenomena of nature as God's acts. When it thunders, they say God thunders. When it rains, they say God rains. When the Christian light shone on them, they did not abandon all the concepts of God they had acquired through their observation of, and reflection on, nature. Rather, many of them were confirmed in him. They received an additional force. They became integrated in their Christian concepts, belief, and practices to make themselves the deeply religious people that they are.

Why God?

At this juncture a fundamental question presents itself. Why did their reflection on nature lead the Buem and the Akan to an ultimate reality, or God, and not to some other reality? Why did they arrive at the concept of God and not of some being? The pros and cons of life, and the riddles of every sunrise and sunset, have always beset the mind of humans. The hard realities of life; the unpredictable and sometimes terrifying hazards of life, such as illness, earthquakes, floods, thunder and suffering, death, the experience of the mysterious forces; all these forced themselves on the mind of the Buem and the Akan and made them seek the source of all power. This was not a mere rational approach to life. It is in the nature of people to look for security and protection in anything that can provide them with it. But if one were to seek security and protection in a baby that was born only yesterday, it would be ridiculous indeed. It is a matter of common sense to turn to something that is stronger than one's self. Therefore, when the Buem and the Akan sought these vital needs, they looked for them in a being which they saw to have special powers that they themselves did not have.

Like many other peoples in the world, the Buem and the Akan ended their search for "who moves life" in the belief of an existence of an ultimate power or reality behind the universe. They knew and felt there was a superior being who owned the world. It was clear to them that such a being could answer the question of who has the monopoly over life. This is the being they called God. To him they gave obedience and worship. One only has to look into the names and attributes given to God—the proverbs, myths, drums, art, signs and symbols of the people—to know whom the Buem and the Akan people understand as God.

The Personal Names of God

The Buem and the Akan have several names for God which express their rich concepts of him. The commonest name by which God is known among the Buem is *Atibluku* or *Atibruku*. The word is a combination of two words: *Ati* and *Bluku* or *Bruku*. *Ati* designates an "elderly man," "Father." *Bluku* (*Bruku*) means that which cannot be escaped from, avoided or resisted—the inevitable. The etymology of this name thus indicates that to the Buem mind, God cannot be resisted. No one can resist his might. The name Atibluku asserts that God is all-powerful, omnipotent.

There is a legend behind this name. It is said that due to frequent wars with their neighboring tribes—the Akan, the Ewe, the Likpe and the Akpafu—the Buem left a common dwelling place. One group travelled to the mountainous area, called Teteman, for security and protection.[5] This group discovered a peculiarly large rock in the vicinity. Its heaviness symbolized powerfulness and strength, so that the rock was associated with God. On top of it worship was offered to *Atibluku*, the Supreme Being who sustained them through wars and perilous travels.

God is also called *Avlukpo*. Although the root of this name is not clear, it has the meaning that God is everlasting.

He is known too as *Koyatu*. This name derives from the words *Kayaa*, which means "sky or atmosphere," and *Otun*, that is, "guardian." The Buem refer by this name to the wisdom and omniscience of God. *Koyatu* means to them that God is all-wise and all-knowing.

The Akan have three principal names for God: *Nyame* or *Onyame, Onyankpon,* and *Odomankoma*. Each of these unearths the Akan understanding of God. According to J. B. Danquah, an eminent Ghanaian author, the commonest of these names among the Akan is Nyame or Onyame. The name, he says, has the same basic notion of Deity in Christian theology.[6] Some authorities on Akan language and culture have given different etymologies of the name. Some think the name Nyame derives from *Nya*, "to get," and *me*, "to be satisfied." In this explanation, Nyame means "the one who satisfies anyone who has him." It is not without reason that I feel attracted to this explanation. This is what Christ tells about himself in John 6:35(JB): "I am the bread of life. He who comes to me will never be hungry; he who believes in me will never thirst." It is suggested that this interpretation of the name God to the Akan is "God of satisfaction."[7] He alone can give full satisfaction and this is because he possesses every quality any being can want to have. When, therefore, one has him, there is nothing more that one needs.

Danquah offers a different meaning of the name—which he considers to be the true one. To him Nyame or Onyame comes from the word *Onyam* (a noun) and means "glory," "dignity," "majesty," "grace." The verb is *nyam*. From these same words onyam and nyam, Danquah says, derives the Akan word *anuonyam,* which translates literally as "splendor of the face," "glory splendor," "brilliancy." He concludes that the Akan root name for God is nyam, that is, "shining," "bright," "glory." So interpreted, Nyame is "the shining one" and the Akan understand God to be the shining one, elevated, but showing himself to humans through his light, brilliance, and splendor.[8]

Let the language experts do their linguistic gymnastics on the origin and meaning of the name. The significant thing is that whichever derivation of the name is deemed correct, both meanings point to one fact: the Akan think of God as a being of a certain type when they call him Nyame. Either he is the one who satiates or he is the shining power.

Another equally important Akan name of God is *Nyankopon* or *Onyankopon*. Again we can only really appreciate the meaning of the name by getting at its etymology. Two main derivations of the name are given. Of these, one readily lends itself to my acceptance. It is the one that derives Nyankopon from three words: *Nyame, Koro* and *pon*. Nyame means God; *koro* means one alone, single; *pon* is the Akan suffix for "great." Composed of these words, Nyankopon or Onyankopon etymologically means "one great God," "alone the great God."[9] By calling God Nyankopon or Onyankopon, the Akan has in mind the supremacy of God. God is the "only great one." God is the Supreme Being, the sovereign God of the universe.

It is worthwhile to point out the distinction that Danquah says the Akan make between the two names. Nyame is God, the Supreme Being who is Deity. Nyankopon is God, the Supreme Being who is sovereign God of the universe.[10]

The third outstanding name of the Akan for God is *Odomankoma*. Those who have tried to explain the root of this name have not found it an easy task. To fully attempt it here would be time consuming. It is generally admitted that from the word *doma,* meaning abundance and hence "the many," "the manifold," "the interminably," "the infinite," Odomankoma means "He who . . . is uninterruptedly, infinitely and exclusively full of the manifold, namely, the interminable, eternally, infinitely, universally filled entity."[11] To make a long matter short, the concept which the Akan has when he calls God Odomankoma is: God is infinitely manifold. He is the infinitely manifold God. He is the immensely rich God, the possessor and, by implication, the giver of an unlimited abundance of things. He is manifold and omnipresent. The name Odomankoma brings out the concept of God as the infinite being.[12]

Praise-Names of God: God's Attributes

Apart from the names described above, there are other names which are used more in praise of God than in calling his name. These signify his attributes and expose his functions.

Among the Buem and the Akan of the Ashanti tribe in particular the power of a chief[13] is seen in the titles he has and the kind of stool name[14] he takes. For example, the name *Odikopim*. *Odi* means "he eats" or "receives something to him," *ko*, "go," and *pim* (*pimpim*), "to face directly." Odikopim means "one who faces something squarely in spite of all odds." In war, such a person does not retreat if he is shot at. As such the name indicates bravery. Similarly, the explanation goes that the name *Bonsu* means "a person is as great as a whale (*su*)," known metaphorically as the sea conquerer. The Ashanti King Osei, who conquered the land from the hinterland to the sea coast, was called Osei Bonsu: "Osei the conqueror of the sea."[15] It is not rare to find a Ghanaian name indicating the role a person plays or has played in life. In much the same way, God has been given names that are manifestations of his goodness, kindness, greatness, power and so on. He is called the following:

1. *Twereduampon:* *twere* is "lean," *dua* is "a tree" and *ampon* is "do not fall." It comes to "lean on a tree and not fall." God is the one we lean on and do not fall. He is our supporter, in other words. When God is invoked, this name is much used. One would often hear *Awurade* (Lord) *Twereduampon*.

2. *Obotantim:* *obo*, "stone or rock"; *tantim*, "unmovable," "a firm or unmovable rock." God is immovable, unchangeable.

3. *Totorobonsu:* *to*, "to fall (as rain)"; *bo*, "to create"; *nsu*, "water." God as Totorobonsu is God as the never-failing copiousness of the source of water. This expresses the overflowing generosity of God.

4. *Berekyirihunuade:* *hunu*, "He who sees or knows" what *ade* "the thing" *berekyiri* "is in front and back of him." God is all-knowing, omniscient.

5. *Ohuntahunu:* the all-seeing God.

6. *Nyansabuakwa:* *nyansa*, "wisdom," the all-wise.

7. *Abommubuwafre:* *wafre* "He on whom you call," *abo* "in your experience," *mmubu* "of distress." God is the consoler or comforter (of the distressed).

8. *Tetekwaframua:* He who is now and from ancient times. He who endures forever. God is eternal.

9. *Akrobeto:* the one you go away from and return to meet. This expresses the same idea of eternity. God is forever there. He has been since time immemorial and will always be.

10. *Daasebere:* *bere* "He who is beyond" *daase* "thanks." You cannot sufficiently thank God for his goodness.

11. *Ahofamado:* the all-loving.

The creative power of God is likewise acknowledged. It is believed that God is the Creator and still active in creation, providing for his creatures. This idea is contained in the following names.

12. *Nyankopon Kokuroko:* literally, the gigantic God. That is, the all-powerful God, the almighty God.

13. *Oboadee: bo,* "to create," and *ade,* "thing." The Creator. It is in this sense that God is called *Osoro ne Asase wura: wura* "Owner" *osoro* "of heaven" *asase* "and earth."

14. *Amowia:* the giver of sunshine.

15. *Amosu:* the giver of rain.

16. *Amaomee:* the giver of sufficiency.

These last three names are a reference to God's providence.

17. *Adomakoma: ma* "the giver" *adom* of "grace."[16]

The praise-names of God are almost countless. All of them give a fair picture of God's nature—his qualities, power and function. This brings us to other aspects of the Buem and Akan languages.

Proverbial Language

Ghanaians have many proverbs, and these play no small part in their speech, especially at the chiefs' courts (palaces). Their importance lies in the fact that they are a concrete and precise way of getting ideas across. What takes a page of a book to be written may take one proverb to be said. A person who speaks in proverbs is considered experienced and wise, for it is said that the wisdom of our elders is found in proverbs.[17] In Ghanaian culture, therefore, a chief must most often speak in proverbs. A good number of the proverbs refer to God. These are a source of knowing about God in Buem and Akan lands as, indeed, in all of Ghana. A few examples are the following:

Buem: 1. *Atibluku olayo efi*—the literal meaning is "God does not like filth." That is to say, God hates sin; He abhors evil. This is God's holiness illustrated.

2. *Atibluku olale*—"God is never asleep." The idea conveyed is that God always sees what man does. Nothing can be hidden from him; nothing can escape his sight, hearing or knowledge. He knows even our most secret thoughts. A person who does something in secret, thinking he is not observed by anyone, is watched by God.

Akan: 3. *Se wo pe asem aka akyere Nyame a, ka kyere mframa*—"If you want to tell God something, tell the wind." This is affirmation of God's omnipresence. Like the wind, God is everywhere. The proverb also asserts God's spirituality and invisibility, for just as the wind is not visible to the eye, so God cannot be seen.

4. *Wo dwane Nyame A, wohye no ase*—"If you run away from God, you are still under him." The same omnipresence of God is indicated. Wherever you are, God is there.

5. *Akoko nom nsuo a, ode kyere Nyame*—"When a fowl drinks water it shows it to God." This is a reference to God's providence and strikes the note that even irrational animals acknowledge it.

6. *Se Nyame nkum wo a, odasani bere kwa*—"Unless God permits that you die, those who try to kill you do so in vain." It means that man's life and destiny are in the hands of God. God is the source and owner of life.

7. *Nyame ne panyin*—"God is the first among all beings. Here is the supremacy of God."

8. *Aboa a oni dua no Nyame na opra ne ho*—"God drives away flies from the tailless animal." God is the helper of the helpless.

9. *Ankonam boafo ne Nyame*—"God cares for the lonely." Both proverbs testify to the providence and care of God for his creatures.

10. *Nyame ma wo yaree a, oma wo aduro*—"If God gives you illness, he gives you the cure." This is God's goodness, mercy and forgiveness. He punishes but forgives.

11. *Akroma se: Ade a Nyame aye nyinaa ye*[18]—"The hawk says: All that God has done is good." We are here carried to the creation story in Genesis: "God saw all He had made, and indeed it was very good" (Gen. 1:31, JB). We know what attribute of God is highlighted here.

It is evident from these examples that proverbial language is one way the people speak about God and make known their religious ideas.

Drum Language

Drums—and here I refer specifically to the native talking drums called *Atimpa* in Buem and *Ntumpan* in Akan—express the deeply religious thought of the people. Talking drums are used to sing praises of God, to proclaim his wonderful deeds, and to announce his qualities to the world. The following song, played rather often on talking drums, is one among the many that can be offered as an example:

From time immemorial
The dependable God bids us all

abide by his injunctions.
Then shall we get whatever we want
Be it white or red.
It is the God Creator, the Gracious one.
Good morning to you, God, good morning.
I am learning, let me succeed.[19]

Mythical Language

Like many peoples of the world, the Buem and the Akan have religious myths which unfold their belief and ideas about God. One famous Buem myth depicts the wisdom and omniscience of God, who outwits *Ananse,* the legendary spider in Ghanaian mythology and folktales who is the quintessence of earthly wisdom. The spider is hired by God to take care of his yam farm.[20] Ananse is jealous of the fertility of God's farm and connives with a rat to sabotage the harvest. He digs a tunnel from God's farm to a big river and bribes the rat to help him carry all the yams by night through the tunnel and dump them in the river. God sees all that Ananse is about, but only laughs at his ruse. After several years of hard labor, Ananse discovers that the river has carried all the yams into God's barns. Ananse then runs away to hide in a corner of his house, overwhelmed with shame. This is why the spider is always found in corners of a room.

A myth known all over Buem- and Akan-land explains God's remoteness and yet nearness to man—the paradox of God referred to in philosophical and theological circles as the transcendence and immanence of God. There are many versions of the myth. The popular version has it that God used to be very near the earth, but a woman was pounding *fufu* (a kind of Ghanaian food) and the pestle hit God. God warned the woman, but still she continued to hit him. So God went far, far away up to the sky where he could have his peace. Implied in the myth is the concept that God loves humans and would want to live with them, but humans would not give him peace. Also, just as Genesis teaches about the fall, implied in this myth is the idea that it was humans and not God who brought disorder between themselves and God.

The Language of Art, Signs and Symbols

In their arts, signs, and symbols, God is spoken about and his attributes are declared. For example, a symbol known as *Gye*

Nyame (except God), which has become so usual a sight as to appear on Ghanaian postage stamps, portrays the absolute power (authority) of God. Also, when a chief dances at cultural festivals, he makes a sign which has the significance of the *Gye Nyame* symbol. He points the forefinger to the sky, and while doing so looks up. By this gesture he is professing that only God is superior to him and God alone he fears.

Conclusion

Our exploration of the religious mind of the Buem and Akan people leaves no one in doubt that they, as indeed all Ghanaians, believe in the existence of an ultimate reality whom they call God. They give him various names and attribute to him many qualities. His name is constantly on their lips in times of joy and in times of distress. They speak about him in every form of language possible—in inscriptions and mottos, on vehicles, doors and doorposts, in proverbs, music, tales, art, etc. A careful study of these leaves one in amazement at the rich mine of concepts the people have about this Deity. It also convinces one of the fact that some of these concepts, to say it modestly, that seem to have come from Christianity are the people's own.

Anyone who knows the Buem and the Akan cannot but endorse what a present-day Ghanaian writer says: "In fact, it would require only a very casual observation of the Akan people . . . [for the scope of this essay, I add, and the Buem people] to discover their deep and continual awareness of the presence of God among them."[21]

Living in Buemland and Akanland today naturally brings home the truth of this assertion.

NOTES

1. M. Francis Agbodzanu, "An Outline History of Teteman Buem (A Town in Buem State) 1700–1977" (unpublished diss. for the specialist certificate in history, Winneba, 1977), 1–15, esp. 13–14.

2. "A Brief Outline of the Other Religions in Ghana," in *Ghana Catholic Diary,* 1982, 121.

3. "History of the Catholic Church in Ghana," in *Ghana Catholic Diary,* 116, also 121–22.

4. Reginald McCurdy, *Who is God: What Reason Can Tell Us* (London: Darton, Longman & Todd, 1964), 32–34.

5. Besides mountainous regions affording by their nature security and protection, it is believed that mountains and rocks are the abode of the lesser gods who also give security to man.

6. J. B. Danquah, *The Akan Doctrine of God: A Fragment of Gold Coast Ethics and Religion,* 2d ed., intro. Kwesi A. Dickson (London: Frank Cass & Co., 1968), 30.

7. Ibid., 31–32.

8. Ibid., 36–40.

9. Ibid., 45, also 43–44, 46–48.

10. Ibid., 46.

11. Ibid., 61.

12. An Akan is reported to have expressed the idea that God is manifold and everywhere to his companion in Akan language this way: *"Odomankoma ye bebree, woko baabiara a wuhu no,"* that is, "Odomankoma is many, and wherever you go you see him," ibid., 62–63.

13. A *Chief* is a King or Ruler, the counterpart of a Mayor in Europe or America.

14. A Stool is to Ghanaian people as a Throne is to Western civilization a symbol of authority.

15. Danquah, 54–55.

16. Many of the names given here are explained in detail by Danquah in *The Akan Doctrine of God,* 40–41, 48–56, to whom I am indebted.

17. The elders are the councilors of a chief or generally people who are advanced in age, experience, and wisdom.

18. Danquah, app. 1, has all but one of the proverbs in Akan. Their religious teachings, however, are mostly my deductions.

19. J. H. Nketia, "Poetry of Drums," in *The Voices of Ghana,* cited by Rt. Rev. Dr. Peter Sarpong, *Ghana in Retrospect* (Tema: Ghana Publishing Corp., 1974), 9.

20. Yam is an edible tuber of a tropical climbing plant.

21. Sarpong, 10.

6

The "Oriental View of Nature" and God

EUN-BONG LEE

An Oriental view of Nature

The systematic expression about the Oriental view of nature in the book of *Chuang Tzu* (莊子) is as follows: "You have heard the voice of *Inrae* [人籟, human flute], but you haven't ever heard the voice of *Girae* [地籟, earth's flute]. Though you have heard the voice of earth's flute, you haven't ever heard the *Cheonrae* [天籟, heavenly flute]."[1]

The disciple of Chuang Tzu, Chayu (子遊), questioned this statement: "I can understand the sounds of the earth's flute that are the sounds coming into being through cracks and many holes on a windy day, and the sounds of the human flute are the voices coming from our throat, but what is the sound of the heavenly flute?"[2]

The most famous commentator on Chuang Tzu's thought, Kuo Hsiang (郭象, A.D. 3), published an "Exposition of the Philosophy of Chuang Tzu." In this he critically interpreted the meaning of the heavenly voices: "All things in the universe seem to be created by the Will of a supreme being, but if we examine further we cannot find such a being. All things exist naturally by themselves, and are not made by any external Will."[3]

According to Kuo Hsiang, if there is any Supreme Being or creator of all things, then all things must be ordered by his will. However, all things are *Jayeon* (自然), that is, self-existing, not *Tayeon* (他然), existing through the will of an external being. In the same way, he has interpreted the concept of *Cheonyeon* (天然, natural form of all things) as that which is not created by any external will.

"The *Cheonyeon* has been naturally formed by its innate power. Why do we call it Cheonyeon? Because it is not made artificially, but formed naturally. The *Cheon* (天, Heaven) does not indicate the blue sky or the heavenly God. It only points to all things themselves in their totality. Therefore, all things can be called *Cheon* and there are no other things outside of *Cheon*. If all things can just be called *Cheon*, this implies that there is no controlling being. In this way, all things have come into being by themselves, not by any other power. This phenomenon can be called *Cheondo* (天道, Heavenly Way)."[4]

Furthermore, Kuo Hsiang maintained that the formation of all things was not achieved through the principle of causality; that is, if *A* was formed by *B*, *A* will be controlled by *B*, so that *A* will be a *B*-controlled subordinate. In other words, *A* will be Tayeon, not Jayeon. If we have accepted that all things are only Jayeon in accordance with Kuo Hsiang's opinion, it is not necessary to set forth any premise as to the forming cause of all things.

As was mentioned before, when the wind blows through tree-covered hills or the crevices of a cave, sounds come into being through the holes. We have called these voices *Girae*. The reason why many sounds are heard through many holes is that there are many things resisting the wind; these sounds are not caused by the wind itself. They are only latent in the wind. Here we can say that the wind itself represents *Cheonrae* symbolically. The *Cheonrae* would be a wind containing immense power from all things. I will thus summarize the Oriental view of nature in two points.

First, the discrimination between nature and God is not found in Chuang Tzu's thought. The ancient Chinese philosophy explained that God, human beings, and nature are closely related with each other. The Cheon that has been a general term for nature indicates not only natural phenomena, but also heavenly God, *Sang-Jae* (上帝).

Second, nature and human beings are not distinguished from each other. It has been called "the Union of Nature and Man" (天人合一). We can see the characteristics of the thought in the ancient form of political organizations. The ancient Chinese established their political organizations according to the law of nature. They believed that the law of nature was controlling the development of all things—the movement of heavenly bodies and the revolution of the four seasons. In ancient China, the Son of Heaven (emperor) performed the season's sacrifice every month. For example, the Son of Heaven performed the sacrifice of welcoming springtime in the eastern outskirts of a town in order to pray to Sang-Jae for an abundant harvest. In this time the Son of Heaven, including his lieges participating in the ceremony, abstained from many things: the slaying of female animals as a sacrifice, the cutting down of trees, the provoking of wars, etc.

The purpose of these abstentions was not detrimental to the *Yang*

(陽, "positive power") of springtime, but was rather to contribute more to benevolent administration under the laws of nature. "The Union of Nature and Man" was premised on the assumption that the common principle connecting humans and nature exists and works internally. What is the common principle which connects them together? According to Chuang Tzu's opinion, it is *Ki* (氣, "energy, vitality or material force"). Chuang Tzu believed that Ki was a basic element, not only in the composition of the body, but also of the mind. In the Korean language, *Kiryuk* (氣力, "energy," "vitality," "spirit"), *Yongki* (勇氣, "courage," "valor"), and *Kiback* (氣魄, "spirit," "soul") have a common element Ki. Ki means a life-giving, animating power. But the most important point of Ki is that the vital energy which is the foundation of our mind and body is the same energy found underlying all things in nature. Therefore, *Cheonki* (天氣, "the energy of nature") is the same as *Inki* (人氣, "the vital energy within the human mind and body"). "The Union of Nature and Man" is possible because of the common element Ki.

The Comparison Between Nature and the Christian God

Traditional Christian theology has been based upon the proofs of the existence of God. The presupposition of these proofs, psychologically if not logically, is that God might or might not exist. They argue from something which, everyone admits, exists (the world) to a being beyond it who could or could not be there. The purpose of these arguments is to show that he must be there, i.e., that his being is necessary, but the presupposition behind it is that there is an entity or being "out there" whose existence is problematic and has to be demonstrated. In this sense, we can say that the traditional formulation of Christianity has been in terms of what we call *supranaturalism*. According to this way of thinking, by which we have all been brought up, God is posited as "the highest being"—out there, above and beyond this world, existing in his own right alongside and over against his creation.

The extreme view of this way of thinking is the Deist conception of God's relation to the world. Here God is the Supreme Being, the grand architect who exists somewhere out beyond the world, and he first started it all going, periodically intervenes in its running, and generally gives evidence of his benevolent interest in it. The whole worldview of the Bible, to be sure, is supranaturalistic. It thinks in terms of a three-story universe with God up there, "above" nature.

Behind such phrases as "God created the heavens and the earth," "God came down from heaven," or "God sent his only-begotten Son," lies a view of the world which portrays God as a person living in heaven, a God who is distinguished from the gods of the heathen by the fact that "there is no god beside me." Here I would like to compare Christian dualistic supranaturalism with the unitary naturalism of Chuang Tzu.

Christianity has a personal God. God is not an abstract idea or a law of nature; as Martin Buber says, he is the personal God to whom we can relate with "Thou." If we pray to God, a miracle might occur. Christianity denies "the Union of Nature and Man." The Christian God as an *otherness* always exists and remains over against the self. But as we have seen, Chuang Tzu did not accept the difference between Cheon and human beings. In Christianity the human soul has been created by God, is not comparable with God's quality, and is only considered as a room in which God dwells.

The Christian concept of a personal God induces Christianity's followers to live by moral actions and guilt feelings, but Chuang Tzu's idea becomes weaker than Christianity. The men who believe in a personal God stand before God in the relationship of master and servants in order to solve their problems. But Chuang Tzu's naturalism has not been identified with morality in the religious meaning; only in the social meaning did it become valid. God has a maternal love, but at the same time becomes an object of fear. The God of Abraham and Jacob insists on the absolute obedience of humans. Humans can achieve salvation by means of unconditional obedience to his command, though they do not exactly understand why God gives his order in that way.

Christianity and Chuang Tzu have different methods to achieve salvation. Christians believe in the dogmas revealed by the personal God. Therefore, Christianity has only one course, to take "salvation from without," that is to say, relying upon the divine will. In this way, an individual can be forgiven his or her irrecoverable sin by God and go to the paradise which is better than and more transcendental than this profane world. On the other hand, Chuang Tzu's naturalism takes "salvation from within." Christians believe in the absolute other, but Chuang Tzu does not propose the *Other* as a premise. Therefore, Chuang Tzu has to emphasize the enlightenment that can be achieved through an immediate intuitive insight to recognize present human conditions with a broader outlook. The root of all evils and miseries is the original ignorance. The recognition that

Chuang Tzu is emphasizing is not new information about the outer world but therapeutic knowledge about his own self, his condition in the world. Therapeutic knowledge has something in common with the way in which a psychiatrist treats mental patients by means of enlightening them about their own selves, their conditions in the world. This therapeutic knowledge involves having a spiritual awakening, perceiving higher enlightenment, and attaining a supreme wisdom.

Western man has emphasized the humanization of nature. He has understood the relation between humans and nature as a subject-object relationship. A human is a subject and nature is an object. A human is a thinking animal, so with his thought he has considered nature as an independently existing object. But on the other hand, Chuang Tzu has regarded the independently existing object as an illusion.

The Possibility of Meeting Between the Two Thoughts

We have seen the differences between the East and the West. Whenever we have brought up these problems, we have come up against an unbridgeable abyss. But I have been impressed deeply by reading *Honest to God* written by John A. T. Robinson.[5] He has renewed some theological expressions. In his opinion, the expressions of "transcendental God" and "personal God" are only metaphors to indicate the reality. The Bible speaks of a God "up there." No doubt its picture of a three-decker universe, of the heaven above, the earth beneath, and the waters under the earth, was once taken quite literally. But we must regard these terms as symbolic language to represent and convey spiritual realities. Of course, most of us know that the traditional language of a three-storied universe is not a serious obstacle. It does not worry us intellectually either, for it is not an offense to faith. We do not wonder how crudely spatial much of the biblical terminology is. But Robinson insists on the break with traditional thinking.

He says that the translation from the God "up there" to the God "out there," though of liberating psychological significance, represented no more than a change of direction in spatial symbolism. Quoting the passage from Tillich, he proposes replacing the images of height, "up there" "out there," by those of depth in order to express the truth of God. He seems to go beyond so much of the traditional religious symbolism when he changes the concept of height to that of depth. We can quote the following passages from Tillich about the meaning of "depth," the ground of our very being.

The name of this infinite and inexhaustible depth and ground of all being is God. That depth is what the word God means. And if that word has not much meaning for you, translate it, and speak of the depths of your life, of the source of your being, of your ultimate concern, of what you take seriously without any reservation. Perhaps, in order to do so, you must forget everything traditional that you have learned about God, perhaps even that word itself. For if you know that God means depth, you know much about him. You can not then call yourself an atheist or unbeliever. For you can not think or say: "Life has no depth! Life is shallow. Being itself is surface only." If you could say this in complete seriousness, you would be an atheist; but otherwise you are not. He who knows about depth knows about God.[6]

The name of this infinite and inexhaustible ground of history is God. That is what the word means, and it is that to which the words Kingdom of God and Divine Providence point. And if these words do not have much meaning for you, translate them, and speak of the depth of history, of the ground and aim of our social life, and what you take seriously without reservation in your moral and political activities. Perhaps you should call this depth *hope,* simply hope. For if you find hope in the ground of history, you are united with the great prophets who were able to look into the depth of their times, who tried to escape it, because they could not stand the horror of their visions, and who yet had the strength to look to an even deeper level and there to discover hope.[7]

What Tillich means by God is the exact opposite of a *deus ex machina.* Here God is a supernatural being to whom one can turn away from the world and who can be relied upon to intervene from without. God is not "out there." The word "God" denotes the ultimate depth of all our being, the creative ground and meaning of all our existence.

So conditioned for us is the word "God" by associations with a being out there that Tillich warns us that, to make the necessary transposition, "you must forget everything traditional that you have learned about God, perhaps even that word itself."[8] Indeed, the line between those who believe in God and those who do not bears little relation to their profession of existence or nonexistence of such a being. It is a question, rather, of their openness to the holy, the sacred, in the unfathomable depths of even the most secular relationship. As Martin Buber puts it, of the person who professedly denies God: "When he, too, who abhors the name, and believes himself to be godless, gives his whole being to addressing the Thou of his life, as a Thou that cannot be limited by another, he addresses God."[9] For in the conditioned he has seen and responded to the unconditional. He has touched the hem of the eternal.

Robinson questions what is meant by speaking of a *personal God.*
Theism, as the term was understood traditionally in history, meant
belief in a supreme person, a self-existent subject of infinite goodness
and power who enters into a relationship with us comparable to that of
one human personality with another. The theist is concerned to argue
the existence of such a being as the creator and most sufficient
explanation of the world as we know it. But what is meant by
believing in God as love? Robinson thinks that to believe in God as love
means to believe that in a pure personal relationship we encounter not
merely what ought to be, but what is the deepest truth about the
structure of reality. This is a tremendous act of faith. But it is not the feat
of persuading oneself of the existence of a superbeing beyond this
world endowed with personal qualities.

Belief in God is the trust, the well-nigh incredible trust, that to give
ourselves to the uttermost in love is not to be confounded but to be
"accepted," the trust that love is the ground of our being, to which
ultimately we come home. If Robinson is right, then theological
statements are not a description of "the highest being" but an analysis
of the depths of personal relationships—or, rather, an analysis of the
depths of all experience "interpreted by love." Theology, as Tillich
insists, is about "that which concerns us ultimately."[10] A statement is
"theological" not because it relates to a particular being called "God,"
but because it asks ultimate questions about the meaning of existence;
it asks, at the level of *theos,* at the level of its deepest mystery, what is the
reality and significance of our life. It is said that God, the final truth and
reality, "deep down," is love. And the specifically Christian view of the
world is asserting that the final definition of this reality from which
"nothing can separate us," since it is the very ground of our being, is
"the love of God in Christ Jesus our Lord" (Rom. 8:39). Of course, it is
not enough to say that "religion is about human fellowship and
community," any more than one can simply reverse the biblical
statement and say that "love is God." But it is right that apart from the
relationship of love there is no knowledge of God: "He who does not
love does not know God; for God is love" (1 John 4:8). To assert that
"God is love" is to believe that in love one comes in touch with the
most fundamental reality in the universe, that being itself ultimately
has character. It is to say, with Buber, that "Every particular Thou is a
glimpse through to the eternal Thou," that it is "between man and
man" that we meet God, not that "man with man—the unity of I and
Thou—is God."[11]

In Robinson's opinion, it is possible to meet Chuang Tzu's naturalism because the question of God is for him the question whether this depth of being is a reality or an illusion, not whether a being exists beyond the bright blue sky or anywhere else. Chuang Tzu has emphasized that the depth of being is a reality, not illusion. To say *Jayeon* ("nature") does not mean that one must establish a "super-world" of divine objects. It does mean that, within itself, the finite world points beyond itself. In other words, it is self-transcendent. I believe that Robinson's great contribution to theology is the reinterpretation of transcendence in a way which preserves its reality while detaching it from the projection of supranaturalism. The divine, as he sees it, does not inhabit a transcendent world *above nature;* it is found in the ecstatic character of this world, as its transcendent depth and ground.

In comparing the two, nature and God, we can conclude that if the question of God is the question of depth of being, not the transcendent, personal God, Chuang Tzu's nature will become a vessel of evangelization. The abandonment of any idea of a God "out there" will inevitably appear as a denial of his "otherness" and the negation of much in the biblical assertion of what Christian theology called "the infinite qualitative difference between God and Man."

NOTES

1. *The Chuang Tzu,* trans. Eun-Bong Lee (Taiwan: n. p., 1967), 17–18.

2. Ibid., 18.

3. Ibid., 19.

4. Ibid.

5. John A. T. Robinson, *Honest to God* (London: SCM Press, 1963).

6. Paul Tillich, *The Christian Century* (Dec. 21, 1960), cited by Robinson in *Honest to God,* 22.

7. Paul Tillich, *The Shaking of the Foundations* (New York: Scribner's, 1948), 60, cited by Robinson in *Honest to God,* 47.

8. Tillich, *The Shaking of the Foundations,* 57, cited in Robinson, 22.

9. Martin Buber, *I and Thou* (New York: Scribner's, 1970), 76.

10. Paul Tillich, *Systematic Theology* (Chicago: University of Chicago Press, 1951), 1:12.

11. Buber, 75.

7

The Buddhist Response to the Idea of the Deity

M. M. J. MARASINGHE

The purpose of this essay is to examine the Buddhist response to the idea of a supreme creator God. It must be noted here that if world religions are classified under three broad categories as theistic, non-theistic and atheistic, then Buddhism falls under the second category, as it does not accept the possibility of a supreme creator God. It is important to remember that despite this, Buddhism does not come under the third category, as it definitely accepts the uninterrupted persistence of a moral order in the universe and, therefore, accepts the possibility and the indispensability of moral life.

In order to understand and adequately appreciate the Buddhist response to the question of a supreme creator God, it is necessary to place Buddhism in its relevant sociohistorical context. Buddhism arose in India in the sixth century B. C. in a socioreligious context dominated by two powerful religious traditions: the *Brāhmaṇa* and the *Śramaṇa*. While the Brahmanic religious tradition explained ultimate reality in terms of an all-embracing creator God who was the source as well as the final repository of all life in the universe, the Śramaṇa religious traditions explained ultimate reality mostly in nontheistic terms, widely differing among themselves as to the nature of their explanations. A few among the Śramaṇas were exponents of atheistic views.

Of the two traditions, the Śramaṇa tradition, being the most ancient in terms of historical antiquity and having stemmed from the spiritual culture of the pre-Aryan Indus Valley civilization, merits our prior attention. The term *Śramaṇa tradition* is used to describe the holders of a loosely knit complexity of religiophilosophical views. These views range between the purely materialistic ones of teachers like Ajita Kesakambali, and the pluralist Jains on the other. However, the most prominent common characteristic of the Śramaṇa tradition, when viewed as a whole, is their anti-Brāhmaṇic and hence nontheistic conception of ultimate reality. They rejected the idea of a creator

God in the same way they rejected the validity of the Vedic sacrificial system as the vehicle of transportation from this world to the next. Heavenly life was eternal and everlasting. Śramaṇa religious traditions explained ultimate reality solely with reference to the spiritual development of humans.

The Brahmanic tradition, on the other hand, was a single composite tradition. The main and therefore the pervading theme of the Brahmanic tradition was their belief in a supreme creator God, the *Great Brahmā*. This Great Brahmā, as described in the Pali Canonical texts, was thus, "That illustrious Brahmā, the Great Brahmā, the Supreme One, the Mighty, the All-seeing, the Ruler, the Lord of all, the Maker, the Creator, the Chief of all, appointing to each his place, the Ancient of days, the Father of all that are and are to be, he by whom we were created, he is steadfast immutable eternal, of a nature that knows no change, and he will remain so for ever and ever . . ."[1] ("*Yo kho so bhavaṃ Brahmā Mahā-Brahmā abhibhū anabhibhūto aññadatthudaso vasavatthi issaro kattā nimmātā seṭṭho sañjitā vasī pitā bhūtabhavyānaṃ yena mayaṃ bhotā Brahmunā nimmitā, so nicco dhuvo sassato aviparināma-dhammo sassatisamaṃ tatheva thassati . . .*" D.1.18f).

The above passage, found repeated at several places in the Pali Canon, seems to sum up the early Buddhist knowledge of this Brahmanic conception of a supreme creator God. The epithets used in this passage to describe the creator God are indicative of the main arguments put forward by the Brahmin exponents of the belief at the time, while what was understood of these epithets by the Buddhists would indicate the basic premises upon which the Buddhist response to the question of a creator God was formulated. These epithets are as follows:

Mahā Brahmā: He is definitely identified here as Mahā Brahmā

Abhibhū: He is the Supreme One, there being no one above him (*abhibhavitvā ṭhito jeṭṭhako 'haṃ asmīti*)

Anabhibhūto: The unconquered. He who cannot be conquered or subordinated by any other being (*Aññehi anabhibhūto*)

Aññadatthudaso: He is the All-seeing One (*Dassanavasena sabbaṃ passāmīti attho*)

Vasavatthi: He is the Ruler, the one who rules over the entire Creation (*Sabbam janam vase vattemīti*)

Issaro: He is the overlord of the entire Creation

Kattā: He is the maker of the world and the maker of the beings, (*ahaṃ lokassā ti*)

Nimmātā: He is the Creator, the one who has created everything, (*paṭhavi-himavanta-sineru-cakkavāla-mahāsamudda-can-dima-suriyā mayā nimmitā ti*)

Seṭṭho: He is the greatest and the highest in the entire Creation

Sañjitā: He is the one who assigns each to his station in life (*Tvaṃ khattiyo nāma hohi, tvaṃ Brāhmaṇo nāma Vesso nāma Suddo nāma Gahaṭṭho nāma Pabbajito nāma, antamaso tvaṃ ottho hohi . . .*)

Vasi: He is the most ancient, the earliest among all beings

Pitā bhūta bhavyānam: He is the father of all that are born, and are to be born.

Nicco: He is steadfast

Dhuvo: He is immutable

Sassato: He is eternal

Aviparināmadhammo: He does not undergo any change whatso-ever.

Sassatisamaṃ tatheva ṭhassati: He will remain so for ever and ever. (DA.1.111)

It is this personal creator God who is referred to in the Buddhist texts and who therefore was the subject of Buddhist discussion on the question of divine creation and divine intervention in the destiny of humans. It must be kept in mind that the Buddhist texts do not show evidence of Brahman as expounded by the Upanishadic philoso-phers. It is important to remember that only a few of the Upanishads, such as the Kaṭha Upanishad and the Chandogya Upanishad, were pre-Buddhistic in their origin. Hence, the Upanishadic system as a whole was still in its infancy and therefore would not have made a considerable impression on Buddhist thinking at this early stage.

It is important to ask why the Buddha objected to the belief in a personal creator God of this nature. According to the Tevijja Sutta of the Dīgha Nikāya, the main objection to the theory is raised on the ground that the belief in the Brahmā was not based on direct personal experience of any sage or seer of the Brahmanic tradition. In the Sutta, the Buddha asks Vāseṭṭha, "Well then, Vāseṭṭha, those ancient Rishis of the Brahmans versed in the Three Vedas, the authors of the verses, the utterers of the verses, whose ancient form of words so chanted, uttered, or composed, the Brahmans of to-day chant over again or repeat; intoning or reciting exactly as has been intoned or recited—to wit, Aṭṭhaka, Vāmaka, Vāmadeva, Vessāmitta, Yama-taggi, Angirasa, Bhāradvāja, Vāseṭṭha, Kassapa, and Bhagu—did even they speak thus, saying: 'We know it, we have seen it, where Brahmā is, whence Brahmā is, whither Brahmā is?' ("*Kim pana Vāseṭṭha? ye pi tevijjānam brāhmaṇānaṃ pubbakā isayo mantānam kattāro*

*mantānaṃ pavattāro, yesam idam etarahi te vijjā brāhmaṇā porānaṃ
mantapadaṃ gītaṃ pavuttaṃ samihitaṃ tadanugāyanti tad anubhāsanti,
bhāsitaṃ anubhāsanti vācitam anuvācenti–seyyathidam Aṭṭhako,
Vāmako, Vāmadevo, Vessāmitto, Yamataggi, Angiraso, Bhāradvājo,
Vāseṭṭho, Kassapo, Bhagu–te pi evam āhaṃsu: 'Mayam etaṃ jānāma
mayam etam passāma yattha vā Brahmā yena vā Brahmā yahiṃ vā Brahmā
ti?"* D.1.238.)

When Vāseṭṭha admits that no one in the entire Brahmanic tradition has claimed knowledge of the Brahma as his own personal
experience, the Buddha points out that such talk of the Brahmins
becomes inappropriate talk (appāṭihīrakathaṃ, D.1.239). Such clarification was very important from the Buddhist point of view, as all
knowledge claimed by the Buddha was definitely based on such
personal realization. The importance attached to this possibility of
personal verification was an important principle in the entire Buddhist tradition, and was always insisted on as in the case of the
Kālāmas, in which nothing was to be accepted on the basis of faith,
traditional antiquity, etc. (A.1.189). With this important and essential
aspect of personal verification lacking, the entire Brahmin tradition
becomes one which is founded on the mere faithful acceptance of a
tradition, the truth of which is not certified. It becomes comparable
to a string of blind men, with neither the former, nor the middle, nor
the hindmost ones able to claim certainty on the basis of personal
verification (*Seyyathāpi . . . andha-veṇi param parā samsaṭṭhāpuriso pi
na passati majjhimo pi na passati pacchimo pi na passati . . .* D.1.239).

Therefore, according to the Buddhist way of thinking, the belief in
a supreme creator God is unacceptable. Hence, Buddhist cosmology
does not have any provision within it for a creator God of any
description. In fact, the very idea of a creator God, according to the
Brahmajāla Sutta of the Dīgha Nikāya, is shown to be based on
wrong understanding (D.1.18). According to this Sutta, the Great
Brahmā was the first to appear in this world at the beginning of its
present cycle of evolution. Shortly after his appearance in this world,
seeing no one except himself around, he thought to himself that it
would be nice if there were to be others like him. When others too
came to the world in the same way that the first being came to be
there, he thought that they came to be there because he desired them
to be there. They too, on their part, thought, since the first being was
already there when they came, that he was their creator or that they
were there because of him. The whole belief as such is shown to be
irrational and unscientific.

It is important to note here that while the Brahmin tradition definitely spoke of creation of the world as a single event, according to Buddhist cosmological thinking, it was just one single event in a series of similar events, there being no beginning either of the world or of an individual series of existence. (*anamataggāyaṃ bhikkhave saṃsāro pubbākoṭi na paññāyati avijjānivaraṇānaṃ sattānaṃ.* . . . S.11.178.)

Furthermore, the Brahmā who was the single creator God of the Brahmanic tradition became just one single individual being among many other such beings. There had been neither important nor indispensable functions that he performed either in the origin or evolution of the world, or in the evolution of human beings. This new breed of Brahmas inhabited eight of fourteen heavenly realms. Thus, the Brahmas, too, formed part of the ordinary world and were therefore subject to the same laws of nature as were the other beings. This means that Buddhism does not accept the idea of a creator God who is above the world and is therefore not subject to the laws of nature, etc., operating in the world.

Thus, the single creator God Brahmā of the Brahmanic religion became demoted in his position as he became just one ordinary individual deity among thousands and millions of other deities like him. Not only this, although the Brahmas belonged to the highest ranks among the nonhuman beings, they were still far inferior to human beings.

This brings us to the most important and the most significant feature of Buddhist cosmological formulations. It has humans as its central concern. According to Buddhist cosmology, the human is the highest and the most important being in the entire universe. All nonhuman categories of life, whether they belong to the realms of the gods or to the other inferior forms of life, are placed far below the level of human life. It is inevitable that all gods, Brahmas, etc., have to be reborn in the human realm before they can attain liberation from the cycle of life. It must be remembered that it is only a human being who can attain Buddhahood, which Buddhists consider to be the highest spiritual development in the world.

As humanity is placed above the gods in the new system of values it is the gods who need the assistance of humans, instead of humans needing the assistance of the gods. This is why the Buddhist texts are replete with details of transactions of gods with human beings. It is interesting to note that the Pali texts record gods, ranging from the Great Brahmā Sahampati—the ruling Mahā Brahmā at the time—to the lowest tree deities (*Rukkha devatās*), as having sought the Buddha or his disciples.

Therefore, instead of human beings depending on the gods, it is now the gods who depend on human beings. The Buddha's very missionary career was prefaced by the visit of the Great Brahmā, who on seeing that the Buddha was reluctant to preach the *dhamma* "message of Buddhism," came to him and requested that the dhamma be proclaimed for the weal and the welfare of the world (Mahāvagga.5f.).

Not only were the gods subordinated to humans, but what was more important, it was shown that it was possible for human beings to be reborn as gods without much effort. According to the Brahmanic religion, much effort in the form of sacrificial fulfillment, as well as material wealth, was necessary to win admission to the immortality of heavenly existence. Such tedious processes were no longer necessary, as one could be reborn into the realms of the gods as a result of performing simple acts of merit. But it must be kept in mind here that though birth into the lower realms of heavenly existence could result from simple deeds of merit, birth into the higher heavenly realms required attainment of spiritual maturity. Each stage in the path to perfection corresponded to a realm of the gods, while the final attainment of nibbana far surpassed all divine existences.[2]

It is important to remember that the majority of the active gods mentioned in the Pali canonical texts are those who were recruited to the ranks of the gods through this process.[3] In adopting this, Buddhism has merely endorsed a historical process which has been operating not only in India but in all human societies in general, namely, the process of deification of historical personalities. Although the historical process of deification required considerable time, this new process brought in quicker results. Individuals were reborn into the company of the various divine realms immediately upon their death. This was how contemporary beneficiaries of the *sangha,* "Order," like Anāthapiṇḍika, Ugga, and even the Magadhan Emperor Bimbisara were recruited into the ranks of the gods.[4] These gods reported to the Buddha after they were reborn as gods. It may be noted here in passing that the Janavasabha Sutta of the Dīgha Nikāya, which is an important discourse, is based on a similar meeting which the former Magadhan Emperor Bimbisara—now reborn into the ranks of Vessavaṇa, the Lord of the lowest heavenly realm—had with the Buddha (D.11.200f.).

It must be emphasized here that birth into the ranks of the gods is neither a natural nor an accidental occurence, but the result of the individual's own express wish to be so born. But the Buddhist texts clearly emphasize the fact that birth into the ranks of the gods of whatever description does not bring any advantage whatsoever to the individual concerned.

The preceding observations make it relevant to ask how human beings become aware of the gods. In other words, these observations lead us to the problem of authority for our views on the gods. As was pointed out earlier, the Buddha, as recorded in the Tevijja Sutta of the Dīgha Nikāya, criticized the Vedic tradition, regarding its claims made about the nature of Brahmā and the path leading to fellowship with him. As K. N. Jayatilleke puts it,

"Here it is said that none of the teachers of the Vedic tradition, not even the original seers have had a direct knowledge or vision of Brahmā. They have not claimed to have 'seen Brahmā face to face' (Brahmā sakkhidiṭṭho, D.1.238) and they did not say, 'we know this, we see this (namely) where, in which direction and in which place Brahmā is' (mayaṃ etaṃ jānāma mayaṃ etaṃ passāma yattha vā brahmā yena vā brahmā yahiṃ vā brahmā ti, D.1.239). Radhakrishnan concludes from examining this Sutta that the 'Buddha does not like the idea of basing the reality of Brahman on Vedic authority, for when once we admit the evidence of revelation there is no end to it' (Indian Philosophy, 1.467). This conclusion appears to be strictly unwarranted by the context, which makes it clear that the Buddha is merely denying that the knowledge of or about Brahmā in the Vedic tradition is not based on a direct vision or revelation of Brahmā at all, whatever the views the Buddha may have had on the validity of revelation itself. The Buddha does not prima facie appear to be averse to the 'idea of basing the reality of Brahman on Vedic authority' provided a valid claim to a real, personal knowledge of Brahmā was made by at least one of the teachers, on whom this tradition was based. The criticism made here is that the Vedic tradition as such is not, and cannot claim to be, a revelation. It is not a denial of the possibility of revelation altogether."[5]

It must be noted here that Radhakrishnan's reference in the above passage quoted by Jayatilleke which reads, "Buddha does not like the idea of basing the *reality of Brahman* on Vedic authority," (italics mine) claiming that the Buddha was conversant with the Upanishadic concept of Brahman is neither historically tenable nor corroborated by textual evidence. Neither has Jayatilleke shown evidence that he was aware of the gap of time between the two concepts of Brahmā and Brahman.

Thus, what the Buddha insisted upon was that our views should be based on direct personal experience. It is important to note in this connection that this direct personal knowledge obtained through a systematic development of the faculties has been the basis of Buddhist views on such teachings as *kamma,* rebirth, etc., as well.

According to evidence recorded in the Pali texts, one becomes aware of the existence of the gods only through transic experience. In other words, it is only through the *dhyānas,* "trances," that the gods can be known. Throughout the Pali texts, it is while the Buddha or a disciple is in a state of trance that transactions with the gods take place. Also, it is interesting to note that the requirement of the dhyāna varies in its depth and in its intensity according to the type of heavenly realm that is to be contacted. For example, a dhyāna which enables one to establish contact with beings in a lower realm of the gods will not suffice to establish contact with the gods of the higher realms. This is why the bhikkhu Kevaddha had to develop that kind of *samādhi* which enabled him to establish contact with the Brahmas (*brahmayāniyo maggo pāturahosi,* D.1.220) when he found that the gods he contacted on his samādhi which enabled him to establish contact with the devas (*devayāniyo maggo pāturahosi,* D.1.215) were not sufficient to reach the Brahmas. The higher realms of the gods thus require correspondingly higher trances to make communication with them possible. According to the Pali texts, it is after the cultivation of the fourth dhyāna that one could, if he or she so desired, establish contact with the gods by special cultivation of dhyāna directed specially with that purpose in view (D.1.151f.).

According to the Anguttara Nikaya, the Buddha's enlightenment was not complete until he realized the eight-fold knowledge and insight surpassing the gods (*Aṭṭhaparivaṭṭaṇ Adhideva nāṇadassanaṃ*). These eight-fold knowledges as enumerated in the Sutte are as follows:

1. Perceiving the auras (*Obhāsaṃ hi kho sanjānāmi*)
2. Seeing forms (. . . *rūpānica passāmi*)
3. Stand with (be in the company of), talk to and engage in conversation with the gods (*devatāhi saddhiṃ santiṭṭhāmi, sallapāmi, sākaccaṃ samāpajjāmi*)
4. Distinctive knowledge of these gods as to the different realms or spheres to which they belong (*Imā devatā amukāmhā vā amukamhā devanikāyā ti*)
5. Penetrative knowledge regarding the gods as to what past deeds conditioned their present births as gods and from having been

what they came to be reborn as such, etc. (*Imā devatā imassa kammassa vipākena ito cutā tattha upapannā ti*)

6. Knowledge regarding their subsistence, their experience, their weal and woe, etc. (*Imā devatā evaṃ āhārā, evaṃ sukhadukkha patisaṃvedaniyo ti*)

7. Knowledge regarding the length of their life spans, the length of life in their present states, etc. (*Imā devatā evaṃ dighāyukā, evaṃ ciraṭṭhitikā ti*)

8. Knowledge of whether he had dwelt with these gods formerly or not (*Imāhi devatāhi saddhiṃ sannivutapubbaṃ yadi vā na sannivutapubban ti*) (A.4.302)[6]

Each successive knowledge in the above eight knowledges results from a gradual deepening of the purposive development of samādhi.

Another important point which emerges from the discussions above is regarding the location of the gods and the heavenly realms. It must be remembered that Buddhist cosmology differs from the cosmologies of other world religions in that it does not concern itself with such problems as the origin, composition, structure, etc., either of the world or of the universe as a whole. Buddhist cosmology as such is properly designated as an analytic cosmology.[7] According to this, either the world or the universe is not conceived of as a storied structure with separate spatial compartments for distinct categories of beings, whether gods or nongods. The realms of the gods are not spoken of as those which are spatially distinct and separated either from the other heavenly realms or from the human world. It is because the gods do not inhabit separate compartments in space that the determination of their group (*devanikāya*, "divine fellowship or divine company") was achieved in the fourth stage of the eight-fold series referred to above.

Another relevant observation that emerges from the above remarks seems to be regarding the movement of the gods. If the transactions with the gods did take place within transic experience, then it is unlikely that physical locomotion was either essential or possible. Moreover, if the gods do not inhabit separate worlds but are accommodated within this same surface, then the movement within the same physical environment does not raise very serious problems. Evidence in the Pali Canonical texts does not support the view that physical locomotion was either necessary or actually took place.[9]

The aim of religious endeavor resulting from the above cosmological conceptions ceases to be an endeavor to attain union or companionship with the gods, as they are subject to the same laws of nature and laws of *kamma* as are human beings. Instead, the aim of religious endeavor becomes one which is to surpass the gods.

Humans, therefore, are not to toil to seek union with the divine, whether by attaining fellowship with the Great Brahmā or by being reborn into the companionship of the gods. What they have to toil for, is development of their faculties in order to reach the highest level of spiritual attainment—which is the exclusive prerogative of humans and humans alone—and thereby rise above all the gods or Brahmās.

It is important to note here that the spiritual cultivation which elevates humans above the gods can only be attained through a systematic development of our faculties through *sīla, samādhi,* and *paññā*. It is the final stage of *paññā* which, upon full maturity, leads to the attainment of nibbana, the goal of the Buddhist spiritual endeavor.

There is no place whatsoever in this scheme of perfection for the intervention of any external agency such as a god. The gods, according to Buddhism, are not endowed with any such power or capacity to intervene in human spiritual activity. Neither are they the centers of any cultic or other religious activity, prayer, or supplication of any description.

It must not be forgotten that the Buddhist response to the belief in a creator God was addressed to a definite religiocultural context, namely, that of the India of sixth century B.C. This would mean that its form was determined by the requirements of that religiocultural environment. It brought in a variety of new gods and new techniques of god-making, all contributing to the nullification of the supremacy of the supernatural element over humans and to raising the status of humans by awakening us to harness our faculties to achieve the fullest blossoming of our inherent capabilities.

NOTES

1. *Sacred Books of the Buddhists,* trans. I. B. Horner (London: Luzac, 1969), 11:32.
2. M. M. J. Marasinghe, *Gods in Early Buddhism* (Kelaniya, Sri Lanka: Vidyalankara Campus, University of Sri Lanka, 1974), see chart facing p. 62.
3. Ibid., 68f.
4. Ibid., 69f.
5. K. N. Jayatilleke, *Early Buddhist Theory of Knowledge* (London: Allen and Unwin, 1963), 182f.
6. Marasinghe, 93.
7. Ibid., 43.
8. Ibid., 56f.
9. Ibid., 94f.

God as Not-Other: Nicholas of Cusa's *De li Non Aliud*

ROBERT P. SCHARLEMANN

Nam etsi primo principio multa attribuantur nomina, quorum nullum ei adaequatum esse potest, cum sit etiam nominum omnium sicut et rerum principium, et nihil principiati omnia antecedat, per unum tamen significandi modum mentis acie praecisius videtur, quam per alium. Neque hactenus equidem comperi quodcumque significatum humanum visum rectius in primum dirigere.

De li Non Aliud

Anyone who is familiar with the theology of the 1920s that bears the name "dialectical theology" and that is associated with the figures of Barth, Bultmann, Gogarten, Tillich, and the like, and who, therefore, is familiar with the conception of God as "totally other"—that is, as other than even the otherness that marks the difference between subject and object, self and world, freedom and destiny, and the rest of the polarities that are the infinite constitution of finite being—may be surprised that one of the main, early representatives of this conception of God formulated it not in terms of the "wholly other" (*totaliter aliter*) but in terms of the *non aliud*. Nicholas of Cusa offered, in his treatise *De li Non Aliud*, a name of God which was to describe a more exact path toward the God who is beyond all names than that offered theretofore in the Neoplatonic tradition represented by Pseudo-Dionysius's treatise "On the Divine Names."

This tradition is characterized by the recognition of the distinction between a reflection on objects of the world and a reflection on language, and, more specifically, on the nouns, or names, that appear in language and that constitute a kind of objectivity different from both the psychic objects of self-reflection and the mundane objects of cosmological reflection. As something audible, when heard, or visible, when written, a noun, or name, has a kind of standing intermediate between that of psychic states or acts and that of physical objects. A name is a thing, but it is a thought-thing. It presents an object to mind, but the object it presents cannot be perceived without thinking the meaning of the physical figure, and that is to say, without the capacity to understand "signs" as well as to perceive sensible appearances and to think, abstractly, cognitive notions. Reflection on names, therefore, or what the Renaissance Aristotelians, such as Zabarella, called "onomatology," is a kind of thinking in which the mind is turned to the meaning that presents itself in the linguistic sign.

The divine names, as objects of such reflection, are intended, in this context, not as designations of objects given otherwise than in the names themselves (as is the case when we coin terms to name new things discovered or produced—like "quark" and "charm" for new physical particles) but as pathways along which the mind is led to the object signified by the names. One has to follow the path charted by the names in order to gain sight of the object signified. They are, as Nicholas described them, like maps leading the pilgrims to the city, but they are not the name of the city itself. The analogy falters, of course, when one considers that one does not have to have a map if one knows the way to the city. With the routes to the name that is beyond all names in heaven and earth, however, the matter is different because they are not only the maps but the routes traversed. As is the case with thought-objects, the one cannot be separated from the other. With physical places, maps are different from the roads they chart; with semantic places, the maps and the roads are the same—the divine names are both the maps and the routes to the destination.

Karl Barth did not resort to Nicholas of Cusa's treatise in laying the foundation for his theology. But he did resort to the kind of reflection that it represents, a reflection on the very word or name that is the word or name of God. It is often overlooked—Barth's "Barthian" or "neo-orthodox" reputation tends to overshadow interpretations of his theology—that in his treatise on Anselm's name of God, *id quo majus cogitari nequit* ("that than which a greater cannot be thought"), what Barth spoke of as the presupposition (*Voraussetzung*) of faith was not the existence of God. Barth did not claim that faith presupposes the existence of God which then understanding tries to make clear or demonstrate. Instead, what faith presupposes is the identification of God with the name "that than which no greater can be thought." And the point of the demonstration is to show that, given this name, the mind, by nothing more than a reflection on the meaning of the name, can arrive at the knowledge of the real existence of the one it names. Barth was explicit in recognizing that the Anselmian-Augustinian phrase involved is not a definition of the essence of God but, initially, the formulation of a rule of thinking. But it is that rule given in a *name*, that is to say, in a thought-object which, when reflected upon, leads the mind to a knowledge of what it names. In that sense, anyone who understands the plain Latin phrase *id quo nihil majus cogitari potest*—anyone who, in other words, can see what is signified by those words—also understands that the one they name cannot be thought of, and cannot be merely a logical entity but must also be a real entity. It was in that way that, for Barth's theology, Anselm provided a means for putting the question of the existence of God behind one, as a question already settled before the theological work is begun.

Like Anselm, however, Barth remained, apparently, unaware of the ambiguity involved in the sense *quo nihil majus cogitari potest*. For the phrase "than which nothing can be thought greater" has the double meaning (a) that "nothing" can be thought, and, when it is thought, then one has thought something greater than God and (b) that it is impossible to think of anything at all that is greater than God; it is impossible to think beyond the one meant by "God." Moreover, even after one follows Anselm's, and Barth's, demonstration, one may see that, indeed, *id quo majus cogitari nequit* must be a real as well as a mental object; but one has no way of distinguishing between the whole structure of the thinking of being and the God who is supposed to be other than that whole structure. It is just this ambiguity, however, that Nicholas's formulation transcends. By virtue of its formulating the identity of being as a double negative ("not" plus "other [=not]"), it eliminates the ambiguity still contained in Anselm's "than which nothing can be thought greater." It also makes a distinction between, on the one hand, the impossibility referred to when we say that we cannot think outside the structure of the thinking-of-being (since to think at all is to think of . . . , and what we think of is, in whatever more specific sense, "being")—the structure of thinking-of-being is for us unconditional—and, on the other hand, the undeniability of the reality and presence of what transcends that structure altogether.

In that respect, this formulation of a divine name improves upon the Augustinian-Anselmian name even in Barth's use of it. In another respect, however, Nicholas's reflection suffers from an obliviousness of "God" in the same way as do Anselm's and Barth's. Here we can see, I think, a remarkable parallel to what Heidegger diagnosed as the forgetfulness of being in the metaphysical tradition. By that, Heidegger meant two different, though related, things: we forget to take account of the very connection between particular and universal that is signified by the word "is" (and hence we also come to think that words may have meanings but entities do not), and we forget that being appears universally and aboriginally only in the form of the first person singular, as the question of how "I" can be the one that I am, or of how "I" can be the "here" designated by the definition of Dasein contained in the thought "'I' am this-one-here." In a striking parallel, the theological tradition overlooks the fact that the very word "God" is itself a name, and hence the question at issue is the legitimacy and sense of combining the name "God" with the other divine names such as "that than which no greater can be thought" or "the not-other." What is the nature of the being designated when one says "God *is* not-other"? or "God *is totaliter aliter*"? "God *is* that than which nothing can be thought greater"? In short, this tradition is oblivious of the *being* of God in a manner parallel to the forgetting of the being of Dasein, and it forgets "God" in a way parallel to the metaphysical forgottenness of the self as "I."

The phrase *non aliud quam,* "not other than," was not Nicholas's coinage. It was current as the phrase for expressing a strong identity between the subject and predicate of a proposition. "This is a tree" does not make a strong, or complete, identification between this thing and the notion of a tree, because, besides being a tree, "this" is other things as well—a wooden object, a tall thing, etc. But "*A* is *A*" is a strong identity, which can be expressed by saying that *A* is "nothing else than" *A;* it is itself and nothing else besides. The play on meanings here—"it is itself *and nothing* else," which seems to imply that an entity is both something and nothing—is also a clue to the way in which this statement of the identity of being avoids the ambiguity of Anselm's formulation. And Nicholas was right in suggesting that this name offered a more direct path to what is beyond being and nonbeing. He was right insofar as this phrasing provides the possibility of distinguishing between "being" when it means being as a whole and "being" when it means the power of being, or being-itself, which transcends the difference between being and nothing.

The heart of Nicholas's argument, or line of thought, is contained in the first hundred or so lines of the treatise.[1] The abbot mentions that he and the others have been occupied with various works of the philosophic tradition—the *Parmenides,* Proclus's *Theology of Plato,* Aristotle, and the works of (Pseudo-) Dionysius the Areopagite. In reply, Nicholas observes that he sometimes thinks they have neglected something that might lead them closer to what they were looking for—"quod propinquius nos duceret ad quaesitum"—and he agrees to the interlocutors' further request to make that point known (*aperiri*) to them. So the conversation is undertaken, and it is done with the condition that, as Nicholas puts it, unless the others are compelled by reason, they will reject as unimportant whatever he says ("quod omnia, quae a me audies, nisi compellaris ratione, ut levia abicias"). That is the "pact" upon which they enter.

The starting point is the observation that what most of all gives knowledge is "definition": "oratio seu ratio est definitio" (1.3). To say what something is, is, in other words, the way in which one most readily (*apprime*) gains knowledge. This applies not peculiarly to the knowledge of God but to any knowledge whatsoever. To come to a knowledge of it is to arrive at the point of understanding what it is. The quickest way to arrive at a knowledge of the object before us is to be told "This is a tree" and then to be told "A tree is a woody perennial plant with one main trunk, etc." In short, to know something is to know what it is. If we know what it is, we also know what it can do and how it will affect us. Hence, if we are seeking to have the truth presented to us—as Nicholas's interlocutors request—then we start with definition.

We might expect, at this point, that what follows is a definition of truth, or of the first principle, or of God. What follows, instead, is the question of the basis of definition: "Whence (why) is it called definition?" or, paraphrased, "Where do we get definition from at all?" or, "Why is it called definition?" or, finally, "From where do we get the definition?" All of these might be translations of the Latin *Sed unde dicitur definitio?* (literally, "But whence is definition said?"). The answer to this question is that it is called definition from defining because it defines all things. Here, too, the answer can be worded differently: *a definiendo, quia omnia definit* can mean that definition is called definition by the very act of defining. Definition comes from defining because defining (or definition) defines all things. That is to say, there is no definition of anything without the act of defining; a definition is the result, or the product, of an act. Defining is what defines everything, whatever the particular definition might be. And a definition of some kind is what defines everything there is, regardless of what the specific definition might be. Definition is called definition because it defines everything; it is called what it is on the basis of what it accomplishes, the definition of everything.

The next step is to consider that, since defining defines everything, it also defines itself. There is a definition not only of all other things besides definition but also of definition itself. The difference, however, is that in this case what is defined (namely, definition) is not other than the defining. Definition defines definition.

Ferdinand admits to following the line of reasoning this far. But he interposes the objection that, while he sees that definition defines itself since it defines everything ("cum nihil excludat"), he does not see what that definition is. What is it that is defined when definition defines itself? The answer is that what is defined, in all defining, is namable as "not other." To define is to employ the relation so named: "A is not other [than A]" and "definition is not other [than definition]." But what is not other? "If," Nicholas says, "with all your might you turn the acute gaze of your mind to not-other, you will see with me the definition which defines itself and everything (quodsi toto nisu mentis aciem ad li non aliud convertis, mecum ipsum definitionem se et omnia definientem videbis)" (1.4.2f.). When Ferdinand then asks for instruction in how to do so, Nicholas replies:

Tell me, then, what is not-other? Is it other than not-other?
Ferdinand: Not at all other.
Nicholas: . . . Then define not-other.
Ferdinand: Indeed, I see clearly how it is that not-other is not other than not-other. No one will deny this.

And Nicholas concludes: "You speak the truth. Do you not now see most certainly that not-other defines itself since it cannot be defined through another (per aliud)" (1.4.15–17).

In the form of question and answer, the discussion can be recapitulated thus: (1) Discourse or reason is definition. But why is it called definition? (2) It gets the name "definition" from the act of defining, which defines all things. What defines it in turn? (3) It defines itself, because it does not exclude anything (it excludes nothing). But what is it? (4) It is nothing else than (non aliud quam) what-is-defined (definitum). But what is the defined? (5) The defined is nothing else than nothing else (non aliud quam non aliud). But what is nothing else? (6) Nothing else is nothing else than nothing else (non aliud est non aliud quam non aliud).

Finally, as a last step in the sequence, not-other is connected with God in the following way. Since not-other is used in the definition of everything, including itself, it is the first beginning, the *primum principium*. But the conventional appellation for the first principle is "God." Says Nicholas: ". . . Many names are attributed to the first beginning (*primum principium*), none of which can be adequate to it, since it is the beginning of all names as well as of all things (and nothing that is originated precedes all things). Nevertheless, the mind's acute gaze sees the beginning more precisely through one mode of signifying than through another. Indeed, I have not previously found that any signification directs human sight to the first more accurately. For just as all things are other than not-other, so any signification which terminates in something other, or in other itself, does not direct to the beginning" (2.6.9–17).

The relation between the two names—"God" and "not other"— is a relation that Nicholas indicates by saying that "not other" is a name in which the reflection of God can be seen by those who are seeking him. "The signification [of the expression "not other"] not only serves us as a way to the beginning but also quite closely figures the unnamable name of God, so that in this signification—just as in a precious *aenigma*—[God] is reflected for those who are searching (innominabile nomen Dei propinquius figurare, ut in ipso tamquam in pretiosiori aenigmate relucescat inquirentibus)" (2.7.24–26).

In the discussion, one question gets treated only glancingly, though it is one that betrays an unclarity in the conception. The question has to do with the relation between other and not-other. The priority of not-other lies in its expressing the pure identity of being; and this emerges in the fact that it is the thought, or expression used to define everything and is, in turn, not defined by anything other than itself. It is more original than other, because other is not other than other, and in that sense is defined by not-other. Of not-other, by contrast, the circle of definition is complete—not other is not other than not other. The subject, the predicate, and the connection between the two are all designatable with the phrase "not other." But if we compare other and not-other, it may be asked whether not-other does not have "other" as its opposite and whether, therefore, there is not something more original than both other and not-other. To this Nicholas replies that the two seem to be opposed but are not—since other depends upon not-other for its being other, it cannot be opposed to not-other (6.21.4; also 2.7.2–4). The asymmetrical relation between the two is, in other words, already indicated by the fact that other depends upon not-other for its definition but not-other does not depend upon other. ("Other is not other than other; not other is not other than not other." Both "other" and "not other," to be what they are, depend upon "being-not-other." The mode of being which aboriginally connects subjects and predicates is "not other" and not "other.")

What we have then, in this line of thought, is an identification of the expression which, when used and routinely understood, is a reference to the same one as the one conventionally called God. The property involved in both cases is that of being the first principle. The first principle of knowledge and of being is thought and understood whenever one thinks the content of the phrase "not other." If we say the sky is not other than the sky, the earth not other than the earth, a stone not other than a stone, then this "not other" is how God is there in the sky. "I might say that in the sky [God] is not other than the sky. For how would the sky be not other than the sky if in it not-other were other than the sky?" And the connection between the not other of the sky and the sky is spelled out: "Now, since the sky is other than not-sky [though it is not other than sky], it is an other. But God, who is not-other, is not the sky, which is an other; nonetheless, in the sky God is not an other; nor is he other than the sky. (Similarly, light is not color, even though in color light is not an other and even though light is not other than color.)" (6.20.15–22).

The kind of thinking employed in following the route charted by the words "not other" is that of speculation, that is to say, a thinking which recognizes in the words a reflection of the reality to which they refer. Like all mirror reflections, this one too presents its referent with a certain inversion. But to think speculatively is to think in such a way as to recognize both that the reflection is a reflection of (it has an "intentionality") and that what it is a reflection of is not presented as it is on its own but in an image that not only represents but also misrepresents it. Nicholas justifies the use of speculation with respect to God as the not-other by the discrepancy between what can be seen *visu mentis,* "by mental sight", and the limitations imposed by the language which, necessarily, we use in order to communicate that vision. "Oportet igitur speculantem facere"—it is necessary to do as a speculator (9.33) when one tries to communicate the *visus mentis.* An example is introduced. "When someone sees snow through a red glass (uti facit videns per vitrum rubeum nivem), he sees the snow and attributes the appearance of redness not to the snow but to the glass. The mind does something similar when it views the unformed through a form (ita facit mens per formam videns informatum)" (9.33).

The comparison with the rose-colored glass, however, highlights the central deficiency of this Neoplatonic conception of speculative thinking. For in the case of the colored glass and the snow, we can see the snow both through the glass and without the glass, and it is this which enables us to attribute the color to the glass and not to the snow even when the snow looks colored to the perceiving eye. In the case of that which is beyond all being and nonbeing and beyond all existence, that which we are seeing through the reflection of language cannot be seen in two ways—first directly and then through the glass. Now, it is true that Nicholas maintains it can. Indeed, that is the point of the mental seeing—the mind's eye can see directly what the understanding communicates through the reflecting glass of language. Hence, the mind can distinguish the glass from what it refers us to just as the physical eye can distinguish the rose-colored glass from the snow which it perceives through the glass. The physical eye knows, implicitly, a rule of translation (even if this is not made explicit) by which it can move from the medium to the object perceived. Similarly, the mental vision must have a rule of translation with which it can move from the reflecting medium (language) to the thing reflected.

But Nicholas ascribes the necessity of the medium to the task of communicating, not to the initial act of apprehension. It is quite possible to see *visu mentis* the one meant by names "God" and "not-other." But if one wishes to communicate the same vision to another, then one must resort to language. Here, however, it is plain that the comparison with the colored glass and snow breaks down. For if we wish to communicate to another what it is that we see as snow, we do not resort to colored glasses—we show the person a patch of snow and say, "There—that's what snow is." If there is a direct mental vision of God, why is it not possible to do the same in this case? I suppose one could rescue the comparison by saying that rose-colored glasses are at first required to look at snow because our sensitive eyes would be blinded without them. Similarly, it is at first necessary to arrive at the vision of God by recourse to the medium of the names for the unnamable. Otherwise our thinking, which depends upon such distinctions as that between being and non-being, formed and unformed, would be incapacitated, "blinded," made incapable of thinking of anything definite at all. But once one has learned to look straight at the thing, be it snow or that which is beyond all being and nonbeing, then one can do both—see it as it is on its own, and see it through a reflecting medium.

Even this concession, however, would not rid us of the besetting difficulty—the question whether the mind's vision is of anything at all, if it is to transcend all distinctions. There is nothing in Neoplatonism or in "*De li Non Aliud*" that removes that difficulty. Here one needs to follow a different course, but one that is indicated even in Nicholas's thought of the *non aliud,* if one follows the Heideggerian clue for analyzing (or "destruing," *destruieren*) the Western metaphysical tradition; namely, that it is characterized by a forgetting of being in its preoccupation with entities.

What Nicholas refers to as the mental vision of the undefinable, ineffable God is more likely something closer to home than is suggested by the idea of what is beyond all form, beyond being and nonbeing, the undefined definer, but as close to home as what is suggested by the idea of what is *in omnibus omnia* ("the all in all things") even though *omnium nihil* ("the nothing of all things").[2] It is the very instantiating power of the word "God" (parallel to the instantiating power of the word "I"). This is one sense that we may ascribe to the notion of the forgetfulness of being—the failure to see that there are some words which differ from others because they cannot be said or thought without, in the very act, bringing into being the reality that they mean. No one can actually think or say the word "I," while understanding its meaning, and not, by the very act, become the one meant by the word. This was the discovery that Descartes made in his *Cogito ergo sum,* despite the fact that what he had discovered was forthwith hidden by its translation into something else. *Cogito sum,* which we can translate as "Thinking 'I,' I am"—or, more fully, "When thinking 'I,' I am 'here'"—was put into the terms of other entities: "I am a thinking thing"; and those terms effectively hide what had really been discovered—that the word "I" has *instantiating* power. Admittedly, this is not how Heidegger himself describes the forgottenness of being in metaphysics. But it is, surely, an aspect of the oblivion that he so names. For there is something about the metaphysical concepts themselves that prevents Descartes from seeing what he has uncovered. To forget being amounts, in this case, to overlooking that there is at least one word with respect to which one cannot separate essence and existence—the very word "I" is what brings into being the reality of selfhood, or self-consciousness. In actual fact, the "I" is then beyond form and nonform, beyond existence and essence, because, strictly speaking, one cannot ascertain *what* it is without simultaneously ascertaining *that* it is and, furthermore, one cannot, strictly speaking, say "what" it is but only where and when it is. Hence, the basic definition of the self is "'I' am 'here-now'" or "I am this-one-here." Though it is called a personal pronoun, as if it were standing in place of a personal name, "I" is not a pronoun of that sort—it is a *demonstrative* pronoun in the sense that its very naming "shows" the reality it means. When I think *of* the "I" of "I think," I am no longer there (but have retreated, as it were, to the position of the agent of that new act of thinking of the self). We can know what the "I" as such is only through the memory we have of what appeared when, in decisive moments, we thought or said, "But *I* think . . ." or "But *I* say. . . ." Hence, unlike the kind of being ascribed to physical objects (*Vorhandenheit,* or "being before our eyes or mind"), the being of the self (the "I" of cogito) is inescapably temporal—"I" am here when. . . .

It appears to me that this, too, is what Nicholas, along with the Neoplatonic mystics as a whole, has recognized in the idea of a visio mentis, though the term is certainly misleading. If it is, then what they recognized is that there is, in the very word "God," the same kind of instantiating power as there is in the word "I." Historically speaking, however, it was not Nicholas of Cusa but Karl Daub, in 1833, who in his debate with critical (or "egoistic," as he called it) idealism made the discovery of the being of God in the word "God" comparable to Descartes' discovery of the being of the self in the word "I." I am referring to his cryptic essay that was published under the title "Über den Logos: Ein Beitrag zur Logik der göttlichen Namen."[3] However matters may lie historically, the point is that the word "God," when said or thought with an understanding of its meaning, *instantiates* what the name refers to. Just as one cannot think "I" without in the act becoming the one meant by the word, so one cannot think "God" without becoming the one upon whom what is meant by the word is shown. "God" instantiates the negative (the not-I and not-this), the other of the self, and of all objects, just as "I" instantiates the self and "this" points out the thing. To say "God" is to *become* the one upon whom that otherness is shown. In that sense, again, God is beyond being and nonbeing or beyond essence and existence.

As these remarks indicate, there is a correlation between the self and God—God is the not-I and not-this, the negative, or other, that is shown upon the self and upon any object. But it might be worth noting, in passing, that it makes no difference whether the "I" is the positive and "God" the negative or whether the converse is so. The one is, in any case, the negation of the other. If "God" instantiates positive being, then "I" am the negative of it; I am nothing over against the everything that is God. Systematically, this represents the difference between reflection (in which "I" comes into being as self-consciousness here and now, and "God" is the not-I) and religion (in which "God" is the positive being over against self-consciousness and "I" am nothing over against God). What the conflict between religion and reflection seeks is a word that instantiates a unity of "God" and "I," a "word of reconciliation," to use the language of Christian theology.

In sum, this first aspect of the forgetting of being, as it appears in Nicholas's "*non aliud*," is the neglect of the instantiating power of the word itself. It is a matter of overlooking that in the case of the word "God" we have to do with a meaning that is also a being; for when one understands the meaning of the word upon thinking or hearing it, one becomes the entity upon which the otherness it means is shown (not-I) and the object to which one is referring becomes the object upon which the otherness is shown (not-this). How a meaning and a being converge in this word I have sought to indicate with the notion of "instantiating"—the meaning of the word instantiates the reality it intends.

The second aspect of the same forgetfulness has to do with the connection made between "God" and another name, as when one says "God is not-other." "Being," in the metaphysical tradition, is just the connection between particular and universal that is indicated by the word "is" in judgments; it appears in the judgment as the "meaning" of the judgment, or proposition, and it appears in a thing as the "reality" of that thing. It is not identical either with the subject or the predicate of propositions or with the particular or universal aspects of the thing, but it appears as mixed with both of them. Hence, according to this same tradition, we come to know it as such neither in the process of perceiving particulars nor in the process of abstracting universals but only in the process of understanding (*intelligere:* reading between) that takes place through discrimination (or analysis) and conclusion (or synthesis). Discrimination sets the opposites apart from each other (the particular, as grammatical subject, from the universal, as grammatical predicate—the perceived "this" over against the thought of the general: "this" [as a] "tree," for example); and conclusion brings them together. The double process shows what it is that we understand when we understand the meaning of being, both as the sense of the proposition and as the reality of the thing. Being is shown upon the thing and in the proposition, but it is not identical with any of the parts of the proposition or aspects of the thing; it is, instead, just that connection which makes the analysis and synthesis possible at all and which is always a matter of understanding rather than of perception or thought.

This understanding of being appears in a different light from that of the metaphysical tradition as soon as one takes account of the peculiarity of the words "I" and "God" by virtue of which they simultaneously convey meaning and present being (in the act of instantiation). For the connection of being that is expressed in the propositions "I am N [= a proper name]" and "God is *non-aliud*" is not the synthesis of a particular, named in the subject-term, with a universal, stated in the predicate-term, but of a universal subject with a particular, or proper, name. Hence, the reflection on the divine names, which in the Middle Ages was often done in the form of commentary on Dionysius's book on the divine names, was not an exercise to pass the time when there was nothing better to do— hoe the garden or reap the crops, let us say—but a part of the effort to know what it is we understand when we understand the meaning of being. Yet the traditional reflection on the divine names, in a second aspect of the forgetting of being, overlooked the clue provided by the fact that the being of "God" is also given in the "is" that connects the name "God" with the other names. This is as true of Nicholas of Cusa as it is of Thomas Aquinas; and Karl Barth, too, retains this oblivion in his book on Anselm by not reflecting on the identification between God and the name "that than which nothing greater can be thought" and by starting with it as the presupposition of faith.

If we do, however, incorporate both forgotten aspects into the reflection, then what emerges is this:

"God is not-other" identifies what is instantiated as not-I with the being of any particular entity. But since any particular entity is, as such, not God, the being of God (as expressed in the "is" that conveys the meaning of the proposition and the reality of language) is a form of being that joins pure opposites. The negative that is instantiated upon any object or subject is thus said to be the same as the being of that object or subject. Any "I" who, in the saying of "God," becomes the one upon whom the otherness is shown, and any "this," upon whose objectivity otherness is shown by the demonstrative "God," are identified in their own being (which is understood in the connection between particular and universal or universal and proper) with God. The being which is instantiated through the words is the being of otherness; the being which is the identity of the things is the being of sameness. The being of God as God is the unity of that otherness and this sameness. In somewhat different terms, and in a different line of thought, this is what Nicholas called the "coincidence of opposites," the falling together within being of otherness and sameness.

But the "coincidence of opposites" does not yet fully identify the being of God; for it does not distinguish between the pure openness of mind to reality (of thinking to being), which is the root of the possibility of thinking of being at all, and the being of God or, for that matter, the (non)being of nothing. For what is it that is, first of all, marked by the convergence of opposites, the logical form of contradiction? What is marked by the thought "X both is and is not y"? The capacity to think this thought is the possibility of thinking of reality as it shows itself at all. If we could not, at the threshold of any actual thought, think, for example, "This building is and is not a house" ("This is and is not a tree," etc.), then we could not make the distinctions and definitions that are part of everyday thought—we could not think in what respects the building in question is, and in what respects it is not, a house (or a member of the class of whatever predicate is chosen). In the presence of a tree we cannot think the thought "That is a lion," if we are to think of the thing as the thing shows itself to our thought. But it is equally true that we could not think of it in its particularity (and still less in its potentiality) if we could not at all think "That is not a tree" in the presence of the thing given positively as a tree. Hence, we can say that the form of contradiction is the form representing the pure openness of thinking to being, the pure form of the receptivity of thought to what shows itself as reality, but nothing more.

The collision of opposites that formed a technique of thinking for Neoplatonic mysticism was intended to enable the mind to perceive just that sheer openness as such—the abyss of being, or suprabeing, or what is supra all essence and existence. There is no reason to consider such techniques as either useless or ineffective; for they can undoubtedly make one aware of that original condition of all science and experience, the pure openness of thought to being. If the Aristotelian part of the metaphysical tradition could ascend to a knowledge of God by the analogy of being, that is, by learning how to know being as such (through discrimination and composition of the understanding of reality, the *intellectus rei*) and by equating God with being as such without asking about the basis of that equation, then the Neoplatonic, mystical part of the same tradition could ascend to a knowledge of God, similarly, by equating God with the sheer openness of thinking to being that is the threshold of all knowledge and by not asking about the basis of that equation. In the case of Nicholas's formulation, God, who is the *nihil omnium* (the "not-" of everything and all things), is identified with the not-nonbeing (the "not other," or the "not not-self" by which all definitions are made) of every entity—the "nothing" is identified with the "being" of anything and all things, provided that "being" is understood as the negation of nonbeing, the *non aliud quam*. By a bit of revealing trickery, the sheer coincidence of opposites can be shown even in the phrase "*non aliud quam.*" Everything besides God is other than God; it is the other of God. So the name for every entity is the name "other." This leads to the definition of all entities: "The other is not other than the other" (any entity as such is not other than something-other-than-God), but "The not other is not other than not other." The not other, accordingly, presupposes only itself for its definition; the other presupposes not other.[4] And the contradiction, or concidence of opposites, is shown in the first words of the basic definition of anything at all: "Aliud est non aliud. . . ." We cannot define anything, therefore, without that form of contradiction at the threshold. (The same can be said about the relation between being and nothing in Hegel. "Being is nothing other than being"—it is not any entity or any property of entities, it is just being. The first three words of that thought, however, provide the condition for the dialectical movement: "Being is nothing. . . .) In other words, the being of God which is contained in the unreflected connection of the name "God" with the name "not other" is the being of openness as such.

The mystical ascent has always been in danger of fleeing not to reality but from reality, and that danger is not avoided in Nicholas's formulation of the name of God. But if one takes a step farther, then that which seems a flight from reality can be seen as a return to the everyday world that gives us the sense of the real in the way it constrains our perception and thought so that we cannot think as we will of what is there but must think of it as it shows itself to us in its givenness. That additional step is to recognize that the appearance or existence of God is existence as other than deity. God is real as nondeity, that is, as the otherness that is manifest upon any self and any thing in the time when the word "God" is active. As active, the word shows the *nihil omnium*, "the nothing of all things," that is *in omnibus* as the negation of nothing. Hence, what the name of God turns the mind to is not a far-off unnamable entity beyond all known entities but any and all mundane entities, each of which and all of which can be the reality upon which God is shown by the word "God" and as which God is God. "God is God as other than deity" is one way of stating this return to mundane reality through the power of the name "God." What the *word* "God" effects is the instantiation of the not-I, not-this, and not-anything-else either (*non aliud*); what the *judgment* about the name of God ("God is *non aliud*") accomplishes is an understanding of the being of God as the sheer openness that is the relation of mind to reality in unity with the sheer givenness that is the relation of actual reality to the mind.[5]

NOTES

1. *De li Non Aliud* was written in 1461–62. It has the form of a tetralogue of Nicholas with three interlocutors: John Andrea Vigevius, abbot of the monastery of St. Justine of Sezadium; Ferdinand Matim of Portugal, Nicholas's personal physician; and Peter Balbus of Pisa, translator of Proclus and, later, bishop of Tropea. The text I am following is that edited and translated by Jasper Hopkins (Minneapolis: University of Minnesota Press, 1979) and based on the edition by the Heidelberg Academy of Sciences. However, I have not followed his translation in many cases. Citation is made by chapter and section (e.g., 2.7) or by chapter, section, and lines (2.7.1–2); sections are numbered continuously without regard to chapter numbers.
2. Hopkins translates this as "none of these things," which is idiomatically correct but does not convey the shade of meaning here; hence, I use "the nothing of all things" instead. The reason will become clearer presently.
3. *Theologische Studien und Kritiken* 6 (1833): 355–410.
4. One ramification of this in Nicholas's discussion is that the most adequate formulation of the Trinity is not "Father, Son, and Spirit," though he permits that formulation because it is found in the Scriptures, but the formulation "Non aliud est non aliud quam non aliud" (Not other is not other than not

other), which implies, as the preceding remarks should show, that the pure possibility of definition at all has a trinitarian structure. (See 5.19.)

5. The God *of* which one thinks, *to* whom one prays, *upon* whom one calls, and *in* whose name one acts or speaks is, then, always God-past (just as the self *of* which I think is a self-past, not the active "I"). Or, to put it more dramatically, the God of metaphysics and religion is always the God who has (just) gone. But the intention of the thought, prayer, adjuration, and invocation is to recall the one who was there when the name was really understood as it was spoken or thought and to expect that one to come again the next time. They are activities of the mean-time, between God-past and God-to-come.

Part Three
CONTEMPORARY QUESTIONS

9

Trinity and Personality

FRITZ BURI

There are two reasons why I have chosen "Trinity and Personality" as the topic of my contribution to the general theme, "God: The Contemporary Discussion." One reason is a more external and occasional one, and the other a more internal, substantial and essential one.

The first consists in the fact that we are gathered for this talk about God on an island called Trinidad.[1] For those who at one time named this place Trinidad, giving it this name was not arbitrary, but happened in connection with their faith in the trinitarian God and with its meaning for their life. The question of what that faith actually was would be an object of historical research and would represent as such a small segment of the long history of the Christian faith in the Holy Trinity, in which the question of the three divine persons and their meaning for human beings and the world were discussed.

In the God-talk of today very little attention is paid to the dogma of the Trinity and its history. The individual of today is interested in his or her own personality and in the question of its realization in the world. Whether the individual takes God into account or not, his or her own personality becomes for him a problem. What is a problem for us is not whether God can be a unity in three persons, but whether God can be thought of as a person at all, and, if so, what our own being (as persons) could mean in this connection. For the individual of today, this latter question is more of a problem than the question of the personality of God—only with the difference that for humans it is not only a historical and more or less occasional question than is that of the personality of God, but it is an essential and substantial problem, one of self-understanding.

Our human concept of personality—to the extent that we even have a concept—not only puts speculation about the Trinity into question; it also, as such, represents a problem for us. In view of this situation I ask myself whether the personality of the triune God, which is called into question by our concept of person, might represent an answer to our question about our human personality. It is my thesis that *personality is the problem of the divine Trinity just as much as the Trinity is the solution to the problem of human personality.*

In the first part, I shall analyze the Trinity in its entirety as being, in view of its historical genesis, a rational irrationality or an irrational rationality. In the second part, we shall recognize, in its dogmatic formulations, symbols of the mystery of being and of the riddle of meaning with which we are confronted by the question of the meaning of our existence as persons.

In the third part, I shall show how the statements of the dogma about the immanent Trinity—the generation of the Son through the Father, the procession of the Holy Spirit from the Father and the Son, and the perichoresis of the three persons—can serve as a symbol of our self-understanding and of our destination to responsible personhood in community. In the fourth part, I shall explain the relationship between the Trinity and the world in the economic Trinity so as to find in creation—as a creation out of nothing and as continuing creation (conservation, guidance, and governance)—in redemption, and in glorification, symbols for the realization of our destiny in a graced self-realization.

As in my *Dogmatics as Self-Understanding of the Christian Faith,* I use here the concept of symbol as an unavoidable objectivation of the nonobjectifiable self, of being, and of the relations of both of them.

I

Let us first recall the basic concepts and structures of the Trinity for which the dogma refers to the *Nicaeno-Constantinopolitanum* (389) and the *Athanasianum* (the *symbolum Quicunque*). According to their definitions the Trinity consists in one divine substance in the three separate persons of the Father, the Son, and the Holy Spirit (*una divina essentia in tribus personis*). The three persons have no essences of their own but they have them in community. Nevertheless, they have their own qualities through which they operate in different manners, first of all in the in-itself-ness of the Trinity in eternity. In this eternal immanence the Father in his fatherhood (*paternitas*) generates the Son in his sonhood (*filiatio*) and from both of them— from the Father and the Son—proceeds the Holy Spirit in his spiration (*spiratio in processione spiritus sancti ex patre filioque*). Although these functions of the three divine persons occur in accordance with their qualities separately (*divise*), the three persons envelop and penetrate one another (*perichoresis* or *circumincessio*).

But the three divine persons do not work only in the immanent realm of the Trinity in eternity (*opera ad intra Trinitatis*), since they are working also in the world in the sphere of time in a threefold manner: in the creation of the world and its conservation, in the redemption of the fallen world, and in the glorious fulfillment of this history of salvation at the end. Although in all these three works directed toward the world (*opera ad extra Trinitatis*) the three persons operate together (*indivise*), it is supposed (*per appropriationem*) that creation and conservation are mainly the work of the Father, redemption the special work of the Son, and that the glorification belongs especially to the Holy Spirit.

It is not astonishing that the dogma assumes for all three parts of the doctrine of the Trinity the basic definition of the triune God, and for the working of the three persons *ad intra* and *ad extra* a supernatural revelation and faith for its acceptance and recognition. For rational thinking the description of the Trinity as outlined is indeed not understandable and not acceptable since it consists in a series of logical contradictions. Although the dogma rejects reason as inadequate for its understanding, it uses reason for the definition of its different parts, and it represents, in its totality, a logical illogical system through an admirable logical subtlety of conceptual differentiations. But it cannot overcome the inadequacies of its definitions: To what extent can persons be distinguished if they are one in their essence? How do qualities remain different when their owners interpenetrate one another, and how is it then possible that they work independently of one another? Is it possible at all to think of a working in eternity, that is, before there is a realm and a time in which it can happen? In the *opera Trinitatis ad extra* after the creation out of nothing, such a worldly surrounding is at hand. But when all three persons are here working together (*indivise*), the Father is in danger of suffering and dying together with the Son, so that the omnipotence of God would be put into question, or so that for a time no God would even exist.

The situation for the dogma becomes even more difficult if one appeals to the Bible as the revelatory foundation of its statements, since the Scriptures do not contain any similar speculations. It is even easier to delineate some of them from the realms of nature and reason than from the Bible. But such secular similarities are taken only as hints (*vestigia*) to the superrational revelation and not as their full proofs. So with the rise of the sciences of nature and history, there remained not only a mystery of faith, but nonsense for reason, so that the dogma was more and more abolished. For modern Protestant theology, the Trinity-formula played only the role of a historical problem, and only the *opera ad extra* were used as a summary of the dogmatics, but without their basis in the *opera ad intra*.

It is, indeed, easy to explain in a historical manner the origin and the development of the trinitarian dogma as a consequence of the process of the biblical-Christian world of representation and thought. In the Old Testament, there is no problem in the relationship of the Creator God and his Messiah, since the latter is thought of as a new David or, in the late Jewish apocalyptic, as a heavenly angel created and chosen by God. As this Son of Man, Jesus probably expected to appear after his death, coming from heaven to establish the kingdom of God on earth in a new world. But because his parousia did not occur and since the history continued, his salvatory work had to be changed by his adherents to the extent that they had to proclaim their faith in the world of the late Hellenistic mystery-religions. Under the pressure of the nonarrival of the parousia and under the influence of their new surroundings, they had to reinterpret the eschatological work of Christ as a sacramental one, which is to say that it no longer consisted in the change of the eons but in the founding of the church as a salvatory institution, through whose sacraments one could attain immortality. But to work in this manner, Jesus Christ had to be deified. The change in the soteriology necessitated a change in the Christology—a double change which is already at work in the Gospel of John. That is, in short, the origin of the Christological debate in the early church which led to the trinitarian dogma.

II

In contradistinction to the theologians, from Ludwig Feuerbach to Albert Schweitzer, who concluded from this history of the dogma of the Trinity that for modern man it is useless and should be discarded, I am convinced that it is still of value for us as a symbol for our self-understanding, a manner of self-understanding in which the original meaning of biblical eschatology can be understood in a better way than in the traditional use of it—not in the speculative Hegelian method through which David Friedrich Strauss interpreted it, but in an existential interpretation of its mythological content.

The origin of the biblical eschatology—that is, of the expectation of a new world as the completion of the present distorted world or as a completely new creation—lies in the problem of the idea of the world as the creation of an almighty good God. For Israel the liberation from Egypt and the founding of the nation by Moses the prophet and leader was the basis for its religion. In this situation Yahweh was for Israel the power of the foundation of its being and of the solution of its problem of meaning. Under the influence of the Babylonian myth of Marduk and his killing of the dragon Tiamat, this national experience was enlarged in a cosmological drama of the creation of the world within which God preserved a special place for his elected people and guided its history. But when Israel succumbed to its enemies and lost its land, this faith in an innerworldly reign of David was changed into a hope for a messiah coming from heaven in the future to solve all the earthly problems. This late Jewish eschatology was taken over by Christianity, concentrated on the belief of the resurrection of Jesus and with the substitution for Israel of the church, for whose completion the return of the risen Christ is expected.

In this manner, the biblical-Christian eschatology is an expression of the being-meaning problem and a speculative construction of its solution. Although its basic structure is dualistic, and pessimistic about the world, it is in its goal not less optimistic and monistic than other worldviews which are in their entirety optimistic on the basis of a total harmony. In view of the reality in which we can find only particular meanings, but not a total overcoming of the meaninglessness, the biblical-Christian dualism is less illusionary than any harmonious optimistic monism, although it is in its final vision not less illusionary. In using the idea of history as the means of overcoming in a supernatural or natural manner the riddle of meaning, it is burdened with the problem of the beginning of history, that is, with the question of the origin of being, from which the harmonious eternal return seems to be free. But as the cyclic worldview does not give an answer to the question of the why of being, so too creation out of nothing does not answer this question. Neither of these two worldviews solves the mystery of being and its riddle of meaning, with which we are confronted in reality when we ask: Why is there something and not nothing, and what is the meaning of our being in the world? Both worldviews are not solutions but expressions of these two problems, which arise for all of those who think about our situation in the world.

Usually we find ourselves confronted primarily with the *meaning-problem,* since it is important for our physical and spiritual life. The criteria we use thereby are not only subjective, in relation to what is meaningful for us; we observe also facts and events which are independent from us in their own relationship of a positive or a negative value. But as our judgment is always relative, since we do not know the whole realm, so too our realizing of intended meanings always remains relative, since we cannot know all the consequences of our doing, and even our best deed has its dark side for us or for our surroundings. In any case, we always have to deal with a *riddle of meaning.* But while in the question of meaning we are dealing only with a riddle, in the *question of being* we are confronted with a *mystery* in which we cannot take any step toward enlightenment, otherwise we would have to extinguish our thinking consciousness, and that would produce for us a night in which all cows are dark. We are not able to say anything about being, since in our necessarily objectifying thinking we always have to do with beings and not with being. The same absolute boundary confronts us in our work, since we are not able to produce something out of nothing but are always dependent on something to create something. Being remains for us an absolute mystery.

To speak of this mystery of being and to explain in some measure its riddle of meaning, we have to use inadequate concepts in which we objectify what is finally not objectifiable, a mythological or speculative imagery understood as symbols, that is, as objectivations of the nonobjectifiable, which have their truth in pointing beyond themselves to an existential reality.

In this manner of symbolizing an existential truth, the dogma of the Trinity in its rational irrationality as a whole can serve us as a symbol of the mystery of being and its riddle of meaning. Although it is constructed by reason, it is said that it can be understood only by faith, that is, by acknowledging the boundaries of rational knowledge and pointing to that which cannot be explained in conceptual logic. To that extent its function is only a formal one, and to that extent it is a basic symbol for our thinking about being and its meaning. Even in this formal, boundary-marking manner, it preserves us from an illusionary natural or supernatural universal teleology and from a nihilism despairing of all meaning. But as we are interested not only in the forms of our thinking but also in its content, so too the dogma of the Trinity is for us not only of formal importance, but has a content which is, for our self-understanding, of even greater importance in view of the opera Trinitatis ad intra and in view of the opera Trinitatis ad extra. First I will take into account the content of the doctrine of the opera Trinitatis ad intra in connection with the positive content of the above-mentioned boundaries of our knowledge symbolized in the rational–irrational mystery of the Trinity as a whole.

III

As was already mentioned when we excluded an illusionary teleology and a despairing nihilism, the *shattering of our objectifying thinking* does not have only negative consequences; rather, it includes *a positive turn,* insofar as it opens for us a new horizon of our being in the world and of its meaning. To acknowledge the impossibility of a universal teleology, and the self-contradiction of nihilism, is to express something that is already more than such illusion and self-contradiction. Even in this negative manner it is truth instead of untruth or half-truth. It frees us from a self-deception and leads us to a positive solution of the basic problem of our life. In the shattering of our asking for meaning in the midst of the riddle of meaning and of the mystery of being, we learn that we are forced to and destined to ask this question.

In view of the inevitable shattering, we would not choose this undertaking; but we acknowledge ourselves as forced and destined toward it. With its problematical form, it belongs to our essence, without which we would lose ourselves. Hence, in the shattering of our asking about being and meaning we discover our real being and meaning, through which we are distinguished from all other forms of being. It is the human personality that appears here, and with its appearance we are dealing no longer with an opaque transcendence but with a special revelation of the transcendence that is knowable not in its totality but in this special destiny of ours—the destiny of being answerable for the question of being and meaning. It is up to us to ask this questionable question, and yet we feel ourselves inevitably destined to ask it and to take upon ourselves its shattering.

To understand oneself as responsible for this undertaking is a special occurrence in the world. It cannot be traced to an objectifiable cause; it is a free decision, for which we find ourselves destined. This destiny cannot be found in the world as a whole, and it is not something that we have effected; rather, it is a special, particular working of transcendence in our self-understanding. We understand ourselves in this manner; but the enactment of the understanding, like the enactment of transcendence, is not objectifiable, but is a nonobjectifiable experience of the working of transcendence in and through us. It is a special kind of mysticism—a matter of becoming one, not with the mystery of being, but with a special working out of that mystery, which can be experienced only with that working.

Just as our self-understanding cannot be objectified in its enactment, so too this special appearance of transcendence does not become an object of discursive thought. To say anything about it, we have to use the language of symbols. In this case, the symbol is not the Trinity in its entirety, which we used as the symbol of the mystery of being and its riddle of meaning, but rather the opera Trinitatis ad intra (the works of the Trinity within itself), in which we have the adequate symbol of the special revelation of this mystery and of the way in which it solves the problem of the meaning of our destiny—the destiny to become a person in community with other persons, to whom we are in relation through transcendence working in this manner. Each of the three modes of operation of the Trinity in its immanence represents a *symbol of our destiny to become a responsible person in community*.

First, the generation of the Son through the Father is an eternal act outside of space and time. As the generation of the Son is the irreducibly free will of the Father, so our destiny of becoming a responsible person is not our choice, and we cannot—without losing it—reduce it to a causal occurrence in space and time; but it occurs itself in the enactment of our nonobjectifiable self-understanding. In the interiority of this enactment, personal being, with the uniqueness of each person, is born. Human being in its essence has the character of uniqueness.

Second, as the *filiatio* is simultaneously the work of the Father and the essence of the Son, so our self-understanding as a person is simultaneously an act of transcendence and our act. We, as much as transcendence itself, are engaged in it. Neither the working of transcendence in setting our destiny, nor our self-understanding in carrying out this destiny occurs independently of the other. In its nonobjectifiability there is an ontological-existential event for which the dogma uses—and this is the third point—the symbols of the Holy Spirit and of the *spiratio*. In enacting our self-understanding, as ones who are destined to become personal beings, we bring about in our existence the transcendental setting of our destiny. That is what the dogma calls the spiration as the working of the Father in the third person, the Holy Spirit; and that is the reason why the Spirit is said to proceed from the Father and the Son (*filioque*). In our personal self-understanding, we no longer have to do with transcendence as such and in itself but rather with the working (symbolized in the Holy Spirit) of its special revelation of our destiny in our inwardness.

Here we are concerned with a fourth aspect of the immanent Trinity: the perichoresis of the three trinitarian persons. Perichoresis refers to the mutual comprehending of the persons in their individual working. It has for us a double meaning. First, in our relationship with transcendence, in which transcendence works only through our self-understanding and not without it, perichoresis symbolizes the distinction between the two. We never become identical with transcendence but stand in a transcendental relation to it. We do have to understand ourselves; we are the subject of our self-understanding. However, even this is not possible without the revelation of transcendence. In our conceptual thinking, we have to go around (*circum-ambulare* [*peri-chorein*]) the transcendence, which remains finally a mystery, never totally unveiled but only revealed in the nonobjectifiable realization of our self-understanding as responsible persons.

Second, this perichoresis does not remain in the inwardness of our personal self, but comprehends other persons in the same way. We must respect them in their own personal destiny, which remains for us a mystery with its problems of meaning. So it is with all kinds of beings which are to be respected in their dignity. This enlarged aspect of the perichoresis leads now to the opera Trinitatis ad extra (the external works of the Trinity) *as the symbols of the realization of our destiny in the world,* and of the world as the place in which this destiny is realized.

IV

In the foregoing, we dealt only with the opera Trinitatis ad intra and found there the symbols for the relationship of our self-understanding and to its transcendence. Just as transcendence is not without immanence, so our transcendental self-understanding also is connected with the world. Christianity formulates this relation between transcendence and immanence in the doctrine of creation, and in the trinitarian dogma it is taken into account as the outer working of the Trinity. These external works of the Trinity consist in the doctrines of the creation as *creatio ex nihilo* at the beginning and of the continuing creation, of the doctrine of the fall, and of the final glorification at the end of time. In contradistinction to the opera ad intra, these opera Trinitatis ad extra occur *indivise,* "indivisibly," or separated from one another.

For the objectifying thought of the natural and historical sciences, these doctrines are untenable, but for our existential self-understanding and its realization in the world they can serve us as the adequate symbols, which indicate different directions corresponding to the specific doctrine.

First, the doctrine of creation out of nothing (*creatio ex nihilo*): This nonbiblical, philosophical, speculative theory, which was originally constructed in order to distinguish God the creator from any demiurges who might need for the creation of the world some material, can serve us not only—as already mentioned—as the symbolic answer to the unanswerable question "Why is there something and not nothing?" but also as a symbol of the essence of the unconditional character of our responsibility. For objectifying thinking, no such unconditionedness is possible, since one can discover in every decision a reason, which has a causal effect, so that the decision can be explained in the schema of cause and effect; and this excludes unconditionedness. We are not well advised to neglect calling responsibility into question in this way, since the unconditionedness of responsibility occurs only at the boundary of objectifying knowledge, whose criteria it must pass through and acknowledge to the extent that responsibility is actually exercised within the realm of demonstrable causality, for in this realm no absolutely new beginning is possible. But in the midst of the relative connection of causal connections that have no beginning or end, human beings have the chance to understand themselves as free and responsible for their decisions, by taking on the consequences, and to bring about a new beginning in this realm of freedom. Insofar as one does not acknowledge a ground of decision outside one's own free will, in which one acknowledges personal duty, humans act in a creative way out of nothing demonstrable. For such an unconditional responsible self-understanding, creatio ex nihilo is the adequate symbol.

Not only the creative effects of this existentially understood creatio ex nihilo occur in time; even the fundamental enactment does so, and it needs for its own carrying out something else, which is not at our disposal, but which must be given by a special working of the mystery of being as an unforeseeable grace. What was true of the existential understanding of creatio ex nihilo is also true for its consequences in the continuation of this creativity (*creatio continua*): we appeal not only to God as the creator but, in accordance with the trinitarian doctrine, to all three persons of the Trinity. The three parts of the *creatio continua* as preservation (*conservatio*), divine concomitance (*concursus divinus*), and government toward fulfillment (*gubernatio*) are, as the dogma says, the common (*indivise*) work of God the Father, God the Son, and God the Holy Spirit, although the preservation may be mostly the work of the Father, the concomitance mainly the work of the second person, and the government the part of the Holy Spirit.

In our existential interpretation of these dogmatic distinctions, we would say conservation means "the understanding of being as wonder." The divine accompanying consists in our consciousness of being accompanied by others in a manner of responsibility for our neighbors near and far—as Luther once said, we are Christs to one another. That is, to form a responsible society, which would be the definition of the true church. *Gubernatio* would then consist in the personal and political realization of such a program under the guidance of this Spirit. This means liberty in obligation and contains the hope of its fulfillment.

Before saying more about this goal, however, we shall have to take into account that not only in the trinitarian dogma but also in our existential realization of its content, the great hindrance to this personal and societal mode of meaningful behavior has to be acknowledged. The dogma speaks here of the fall and its consequences. We understand these doctrines as symbols for the possibility that we might miss our destiny through outer or inner failings. In view of this problematic human situation, Christianity proclaims the saving work of Christ in his preaching, vicarious atoning death, and his resurrection, in which the content of the second trinitarian opus ad extra consists, namely, of redemption.

Here is not the place to develop the different stations of the redemptive work of Christ as the Son of God, in whose passion and death even the Father is involved. We content ourselves with the existential interpretation of this mythology as a symbol of the saving insight and acceptance of our guilt, for the possibility of its expiation through our own atonement, and the regaining of our lost identity as a resurrection from spiritual death.

As creation out of nothing goes on in continuing creation, so too redemption works in our individual and collective history toward its fulfillment in the final glorification, which is the third opus Trinitatis ad extra. In it we find not only the symbols for the meaning of culture and its history, for its decay and its judgment, but also for the hope which is included in responsibility, since we have the right to hope to the extent that we carry out our destiny of unconditional responsibility in community. In each moment of such a personal realization there occurs the final judgment, and a new creation of our world in which we find a full compensation for an illusionary history of salvation, as it is called; and a pseudo-futurology is turned into the actualization of a real eschatology.

In this way we can free the biblical-Christian eschatology from the fallacy in which we found the origin of the doctrine of the Trinity. With the symbols of this doctrine, however, we are able to overcome the historical problems of the understanding of the doctrine, when we understand the *Trinity as the symbol of personality.*

Let us conclude with an allusion to a special matter in the last treated opus Trinitatis ad extra. Although dogmatics stresses the indivisible character of these outer works, it does permit one to speak of the creation *per appropriationem,* "by approximation," as the work of the Father, and of the redemption as the work of the Son, and of the glorification as the work of the Holy Spirit. We should like to enlarge this appropriation of these main Christian doctrines and apply it to the trinitarian schemes of other religions, in the Buddhist Trikaya or in Trimurti of the Hindus. We would especially say about Christ what is said in the Bhagavad Gita about Krishna: "in whatever name a person venerates me, if he does so with all his heart, it is all right." In our terminology that means: he does it in unconditional personal responsibility in community with the transcendental relationship to the special mystery of being and its riddle of meaning as it is symbolized in the symbol of the triune God.

My essay, in its methodological importance, could be summarized in the following thesis: In the encounter of the different beliefs in God and of their negations, we do not have to insist on their positive or negative positions, but we do have to bring together the problems of both of them and interpret these positions as expressions of the basic problem of being and its riddle of meaning, which cannot be solved in objective thinking, but only in existentially understood symbols in whose hermeneutical dialectic the God-problem reveals itself as the problem of becoming human.

NOTES

1. The conference was originally scheduled to take place on that island. [Ed.]

10

The Doctrine of the Trinity—Is It Relevant for Contemporary Christian Theology?

MERCY AMBA ODUYOYE

Introduction

In the current search for meaningful ways in which to express the Christian faith, there have been broadly two ways of facing the task: dogmatics and problematics. Dogmatic theologians have opted for maintaining the classical statements of the faith, as embodied in the Chalcedonian Definition, as a point of departure. Some construe the task as one of reformulating the dogma in order to make it comprehensible, for both the structure and the content are divinely revealed and therefore permanently valid; others question even the fundamentals of those classical statements, asking whether the formulas handed down to us really fit the seminal experience that generated them. Thus, in the field of dogmatics, contemporary theologians are at work reexamining the basic tenets of Christianity.

The other type of theology on the contemporary scene, the "problematics," John Hick says, ". . . takes place at the interfaces between the tradition and the world—both the secular world and the wider religious world—and is concerned to create new theology in the light of new situations."[1] The latter of course does not ignore the former; neither is the former prosecuted only as part of the intellectual gymnastics that academia is often accused of indulging in. If it is, it will cease to be theology, for theology is no less than our attempt at giving a reasoned expression to our belief in God, and that we have to do in this body and in this world, although it is related to our "ultimate concern."

Contemporary Theology

Contemporary Christian theology addresses itself to both dogmatics and problematics. In recent times the former has hit the headlines in publications like J. A. T. Robinson's *Honest to God* and John Hick's *The Myth of the Incarnate God,* while the latter has been highlighted in James Cone's *God of the Oppressed,* Gustavo Gutierrez's *Theology of Liberation,* Basil Moore's *Black Theology, A South African Voice* and others. On both fronts several theological issues have been raised which demand further elaboration in forms that take account of people's histories, both communal and individual.

In Africa, the issues of "salvation and liberation," "creation, ecology and stewardship," and "racism and the unity of humankind" are all being explored. All over the world, the proximity of the world religions has raised, in new and fascinating ways, the question of the "uniqueness" (or otherwise) of Jesus Christ in world history, while the renewed interest in the "personhood of the woman" puts a question mark not only on beliefs and practices but on the relation between the two. It is evident that whether dogmatic or problematic, Christian theology applies itself to the basic beliefs of Christianity.

Matter of Relevance

The concern for the indigenization of Christianity in Africa has meant for most the adaptation of its practices to African ritual and forms. It is therefore not surprising that a doctrine of God that declares a sharing of enterprise as well as of glory becomes burdensome when translated into human relations. Nevertheless, this is precisely the point at which the doctrine, fuzzy as it is, should be studied, understood, and lived. The divine economy (*oikonomia,* "the way in which God is organized for a particular purpose") ought to be approximated in human relations.

Living Out the Trinitarian Life

One thing I have gathered from the gospels is this: Jesus came with a unique way of looking at the world. He spoke and lived a life which declared that the only reality in this world is God. He taught that all our attempts at securing ourselves, our self-concern (or it is selfishness?) are basically atheistic. Bultmann would say it is the original sin.[2] Jesus was insistent that the *only* way out of this is to lose ourselves; that is the only condition for securing true life. This is a completely new perspective on human life. It is a radical departure from what unredeemed human nature would recommend. It envisages a new creation. For this to begin to happen the world needed a movement of healing and restoration. Christianity claims to be such a movement; it claims to embody the "faith of Jesus."[3]

It is from this stand that I view the ethical function of the Trinity. Living a life of faith in God demands a radical reassessment of where our salvation lies. This includes preeminently a reconception of the importance of *self* and our well-being as individuals. I submit that a life of faith in God demands participation at all levels for all. This is a style of life that calls for cooperation rather than determined attempts to succeed on one's own. The truth of what Jesus has said about the world and God is not something one can expect others to accept simply because this is what they have been taught. They will only come to know as they begin to take steps to walk "The Way." Our relationship to truth cannot be theoretical. The question then is this: Can a group of people function in such a way that while not being submerged as individuals, there will exist such a concerted atmosphere that one can live for all and all for one? We see in the Godhead how "several centers of consciousness are integrated with and related to one another."[4] We find the Persons in a constant and perfect mutual relationship and we are reminded of the need for properly adjusted relationships in our human families, institutions, and nations. Hodgson asks us to see the doctrine of the Trinity as "a distinction of Persons with a closeness of unity characteristic of modes of existence."[5] In this way both the unity and the diversity in a community will be seen as being equally important.

Traditionally, as we have seen, the doctrine was a response to the fact that the early Christians could not "reduce" all of God to the "human incarnation" and yet they were convinced of his Lordship. Could this say something to our political problems of the relative standing of the individual in a community? "The community of Three" in the one Godhead is certainly more than Father plus Son plus Spirit; each is distinct and yet the community is a reality because of the way in which it functions—so much so that the Augustinian formula *"opera trinitatis ad extra sunt indivisa"* originally spearheaded by the Cappadocian fathers became central in post-Nicene theology. Basil would say, "It is the names that distinguish them not the activities for in that, they are perfectly indistinguishable."[6] (I observed this in my relationship with my parents, so did the other children—we nicknamed the syndrome "The Echo.")

In the Son, the Trinity shared and continues to share the suffering and evil of this world, just as in the Spirit the Godhead continues to be our constant guide into all truth. Following an analogy downwards one can say that it is only in community that our humanity means anything. Experiencing Jesus was for the disciples an experience of God's own self-revelation, and the spirit that guided their lives they described as the spirit of God. What does this say to life in our human community?

There is a hint of a political theory to be formulated out of what Bankway has to say on the Trinity when he thinks of the practical value of the doctrine:

The manifoldness of the divine nature contains the treasure and truth after which polytheism was grasping in its array of many Gods. . . . Similarly . . . the opposite truths expressed by Deism, with its emphasis on the absolute transcendence of God, and Pantheism, with its insistence on His all-pervasive presence. [7]

The constitutions of federal governments are illustrative of the human search for a just balance of the "one and the many." The model of polytheism (making diverse gods out of Deity) produces situations of anarchy because individuals place emphasis on *their* powers, *their* rights, and *their* needs. That is what can happen to states in a federation. On the other hand, structures and systems that claim to be all pervasive are bound to create rancor when they operate at cross-purposes with the aspirations of the units of which they are made up. We even have examples of countries "that run themselves," i. e., in which politics seem to play a minimal role and "business" runs the show. Such a system, impersonal and bureaucratic, may result in such uniformity as makes human life dull and meaningless. The Trinitarian model is full of vitality; the energy is generated by love, participation, and sharing. It is a model which gives further meaning to our being created in the image of God.

At the Bangalore meeting of the "Commission On Faith and Order," in 1978, Metropolitan Mar Osthathios, commenting on the first draft of the message from the commission, had this to say: "The unity of humanity is to be modelled on Trinitarian unity. . . . Ultimately all differences and separations between human beings have to be dissolved in a mutual *perichoresis* (embracing, penetrating, not merely sharing) where 'thine and mine' are not different in case of property, purpose and will but different only in different personal and group identities with full openness to and penetration of each other. . . . The mystery of the unity of humanity in Christ, patterned on the mystery of the Triune unity in the Godhead, has high significance for our social goals also. . . . Ultimately, parochialism, insularity, division, separation, class, ethnic conflict, political and economic injustice, exploitation and oppression have to be judged by this criterion!"[8]

The struggle to hammer out sociopolitical ideologies capable of undergiving and inspiring our life together has been bedeviled with all sorts of "isms." In the above statement I see an attempt to spell out the meaning and practice of the *Sensus Communis* as understood (if not fully practiced) in "traditional" Africa.

The oldest form of human "isms"—sexism—was also examined at Bangalore. The German theologian Jan Milie Lochman, giving the report of one preparatory meeting, had this to say: "The Unity-in-diversity of the Holy Trinity points to true community. God is One and Unbroken, yet has relationships among the Three persons, God relates inwardly and outwardly. . . . Likewise human communities have unity, yet they must encompass diversity."[9] He was reporting on "Discipline of Communion in a divided world of Women and Men." Christian theology has not simply presented the Trinity as a more adequate metaphysical symbol of Deity, but has attempted to demonstrate its symbolic value as a model for human relationships. In this respect the relevance of the doctrine for contemporary theology becomes apparent. But Christian doctrines have relevance not only on the horizontal. We therefore have to drop the plumline against our vertical relations to the Deity.

The Trinity and the Sacraments

Our baptism into the name of the Trinity should mean that we stand not for monarchies and hierarchies but rather for participation.[10] In God's economy we find a sharing of power and a sharing of responsibility, the outcome of which is attributed to all. The unity that exists in the Trinity does not have easy analogies in creation—both the threeness and the oneness are different from anything we know in finite society. Nevertheless, the principles of analogy and of symbolic language allow us the latitude of hoping that human society can at least try to get rid of the kind of distinctions that kill attempts at unity and eventually commit suicide.

Our baptism into the name of the Trinity also means that we share Jesus's acceptance of solidarity with sinners which led him on a path of self-giving—not just on behalf of the baptized, but of the whole world. Through baptism we take part in the Trinitarian economy toward the salvation of the whole world. So much for baptism.

In the Eucharist we give thanks to the Blessed Trinity for creating, redeeming, sanctifying and for all other benedictions that the whole creation receives at the hands of the "Three-in-One." We give praise on behalf of the whole world, which God has reconciled to himself. In the *Anamnetic* aspect of the sacrament, we focus specifically on God, the Son, and in the *Epiklesis* we pray for the Holy Spirit. In the Eucharist we demonstrate our faith in the unity and diversity that is God. In this act of worship we also find communion as Christians, as well as representing the goal of salvation, namely, the fulfillment of the Kingdom. If this is so, then the Eucharist should mean that the world is the church's business. But should it not also mean that both the unity and the diversity that is the church are God-given? Shall we not emphasize diversity rather than division and replace wholeness with the uniformity we seek? It seems to me that the ability to sing the *Doxology* depends on our saying "Yes" to diversity.

The Oneness of the Church

In recent times both the World Council of Churches and the Vatican have reiterated what the Eastern Orthodox churches always maintained, that the ground and the goal of the church is the Blessed Trinity.[11] One can on this ground go to the doctrine of the Trinity to see if it can enable us to disentangle our conceptions of the unity of the church. The Cappadocians, in their attempt to incorporate the ideas of the full substantial divinity of the Son and the Spirit into the old pattern of monotheism, did so by modifying the idea of unity. As platonists they insisted that the unity of divine activity is evidence against any division of the divine *ousia*. The church accepted this. But was the church ready to apply this differentiated unity of God to itself? It is not until modern times that the church has begun to think in terms of organic unity. Previously, the goal seems to have been the organizational unity of the church, not only in each place but even universally.

Take the baptismal controversy that followed the Decian persecution. Cyprian would not accept Novatianist baptism because he reckoned that the church, of which *he* was the head, was the only church. He appealed to Rome in a bid to make his stand the

Catholic policy, but Stephen of Rome was of a different opinion. He recognized a differentiated unity as far as validity of sacraments was concerned. Thus he gave us a principle that the Christian who disagrees with you is not necessarily a heathen. Later bishops of Rome were not so liberal. Augustine too recognized Donatist baptism and ordination. On this account, should not the Cyprianic concept of unity of the church be modified?

If Augustine could tell the Donatists that the holiness of the church is eschatological, why did he refuse to say that true unity of the church is also eschatological? Why did he take his stand with Cyprian on empirical unity defined as one organization? Should the organic unity of the Trinity, which we confess (although we do not fully understand), not make us tolerant of the idea of organic unity of the church? Should our confession of the unity of activity of the Trinity toward the world not steer the church toward unity of action toward and on behalf of the world?

The church, we all agree with O'Neill, "is the one body of Christ (mystically constituted) in which members have union and are united by the sacraments" (baptism and Eucharist). Of course the diversity is more evident. Diversity of members, offices, mode of worship, organizations, etc., exist. Is it too much to claim that all this is geared toward common purpose by the Spirit and by charity.

Conclusion

It is much "easier" to write the doctrine off as "nonsense," a mystery, a metaphysical puzzle, even as blasphemy, than to attempt to see what I think is being revealed through this expression of faith. To confess the reality on which it is based is to discover what I believe to be a valid basis on which we can live truly human lives, something for which we are clearly not ready. Not just as individuals, but as families, institutions, nations, and *churches*. Not even the primitive church that struggled with formulating the doctrine was ready for its implications. All our human organizations are convicted by the standards of the "Trinitarian Community."

If the church lives out the implications of the Trinity, Christians will have no problem with claiming that the doctrine is relevant, even though inexplicable. The doctrine will be seen as being important for the understanding of reconciliation, redemption, and for the fulfillment of humanity after the shape of the Godhead. I am not saying that the doctrine of the Trinity is indispensable, although others have died for it. What I am saying is this: "Now we see through a glass darkly. . . ."

=== NOTES ===

1. John Hick, *God Has Many Names* (London: Macmillan, 1980), 1.

2. Dorothe Soelle, *Political Theology,* trans. John Shelly (Philadelphia: Fortress Press, 1969), 60.

3. Alex Vidler, *Objections to Christian Belief* (London: Constable, 1963), 106.

4. David Brown, *The Divine Trinity* (London: Sheldon Press, 1969), 60.

5. Leonard Hodgson, "The Doctrine of the Trinity: Some Further Thoughts," *J. T. S.,* n. s., 5 (1954): 45.

6. Maurice F. Wiles, *The Making of Christian Doctrine* (Cambridge: Cambridge University Press, 1967), 128. One cannot but agree with Wiles that this is modalism and that the only way to avoid this pitfall is to say, "It has been imparted to us as a verbal disclosure about the inner nature of the godhead in Scripture or the apostolic Tradition."

7. Lumsden Barkway, *The Creed and its Credentials* (London: S. P. C. K., 1957), 75.

8. The official report of this meeting is published by The World Council of Churches in Faith and Order Paper No. 92: *Sharing in One Hope.* See pp. 1–11 for the final form of the message.

9. Ibid.

10. I have taken a position which is hotly debated when applied to human community especially to the organization of the Church. See Austin Flannary, O. P., ed., *Vatican II The Church Constitution* (Dublin: Scepter Books, n. d.), chap. 3, contributed by Cornelius Williams, O. P.

11. Ibid., 22–42; cf. *One Lord, One Baptism,* World Council of Churches Faith and Order Document (London: Student Christian Movement Press, 1960), 12–44.

11

Language and Ontology: The Ontological Structure Within the Biblical Language About God
THOR STEINER GRÖDAL

People speak about God in different ways, and there are varieties of concepts of Deity. When different people use the word "God," they can be assuming such different meanings that one wonders if the word is possible to use at all. I think the situation would be clearer and the discussion more fruitful if we learned to see the connection between different types of ontology (theories of what there is, what kind of reality we live in) and the different meanings of the word "God." One's language about ultimate reality will tell a great deal about the way one's concept of Deity will have to be understood. Therefore, a thinking Christian should learn to discern what kind of ontology is implied in different ways of thought and speech, and, even more important, to see what kind of ontological structure the Bible displays.

Paul Tillich

One theologian who has been keenly aware of the importance ontology plays in one's thinking is Paul Tillich.[1] In his writings he develops his theology on the basis of a clearly exposed ontological discussion. Tillich may therefore serve as a good introductory example of how the ontological structure gives the key to a valid understanding of the names and concepts of Deity employed.

The point of departure in Tillich's thinking is a certain concept of the totality of reality. This concept is understood dialectically, in the relation between the unconditional and the conditional, between transcendence and immanence, and between the infinite and the finite. He speaks of two correlating, interdependent spheres of reality; the temporal/secular and the eternal/theological, both belonging to one and the same reality.

This correlation takes place only where questions in human

existence refer to the ultimate concern—the question of being or nonbeing, what it means to be. This concern is ultimate because it concerns the unconditional and because it deals with our total existence, its structure, meaning, and goal. From this concern no one can escape. The unconditional cannot be fixed as an object of thought. If so, it would be placed within finite space-time categories, and lose its unconditional status. Rather, it shows itself through each individual *within* his or her ultimate concern. Therefore one cannot give any objective criteria of what being itself means. The ultimate can be described in a formal way only.

Ultimate reality, i. e., being, is dialectical, because the structure of human existence, as participating in being, is dialectical. The polar relationship between the conditional/temporal and the unconditional/eternal is consequently dialectical, too. This dialectic, however, is dynamic and forms a synthesis—being, which encompasses the opposite poles and brings them together in harmony. Because being is the highest principle, and because everything participates in harmony and oneness here, correlation between the individual and the universal is possible.

Tillich's concept of total reality is transcendental; it covers everything. A revelation cannot bring forth anything really "new," but only make known being's hidden, but already existent, potentialities. God must be placed within this ontology; there is no room for him to come in from the "outside." How, then, does Tillich talk about God? In Protestant theology God is the creator and sustainer of the entire universe. One must not identify him, the supreme, with anything created. Tillich's interpretation is to equate him with unconditional being. This means that God cannot be spoken of as an object except in mythological, symbolical form. Reducing God to an object of thought is to commit idolatry. The ultimate, God, concerns the depth in our existence, the ground of being, not an existent idea, thing, or person.

The Christian revelation shows mystery to the self-estranged individual;[2] the secret of being is exemplified through "the new being" of Christ. But this dimension transcends the subject-object structure, which is why it cannot be expressed in subject-object categories. Revelation must necessarily take the form of myth and symbol, as these are meant to transcend the subject-object structure. Humans and God are reunited, as individual and universal being are reunited, in being itself. This happens as individuals in their attitude of ultimate concern receive God's word.

What exactly God's word says, however, is impossible to describe in subject-object language, as God's word talks about the ground of being *within* all there is. How then do we know when we have received God's word correctly, been reunited with God? This too is impossible to describe within subject-object categories. It is up to each individual to subjectively decide for him or herself what it means, as well as whether it has happened or not. Besides the formal description of a dynamic dialectic, there are no criteria of content. Therefore, Tillich's names and concepts of Deity can be interpreted in quite different ways. There is no restriction within his system to exclude pantheistic (of a dynamic rather than static type) or even pure secular interpretations of his language. This is so because being can survive as an ultimate concern (not being developed further through a new antithesis-synthesis) only if it is given no descriptive content whatsoever. The names and concepts of Deity might ultimately be nothing more than a linguistic superstructure upon the basis of secular, materialistic constituencies. In other words, God might be non-God, or rather—anything. "Tillich's theology is indeed safe from anti-theological arguments, . . . but only at the expense of *being compatible with anything whatever.*"[3]

These points are made not to argue against Tillich's ontology as such. It is a way of thinking that deserves great respect and thorough examination, as it belongs to the body of profound existentialist and Eastern answers to basic ontological questions.[4] My aim here is to show the connection between Tillich's ontology and his concept of Deity.

The Biblical Ontological Structure

The important question now is to consider if this philosophical ontology equals biblical ontology as Tillich proposes, or whether they form two opposites which no dialectic can harmonize without destroying at least one of the two. In talking about *the* biblical ontology, I presuppose two things. First, "The meaning of a text is linguistic and communal, or as Hirsch says, can be reproduced in more than one consciousness, and it is normatively identical with what the author meant by the particular linguistic symbols he employed."[5] Secondly, I presuppose that the content of the Bible is coherent. Within which ontological structure, then, does the Bible talk about God?

The concept of revelation in the New Testament is connected to the human inability of self-transcendence. God is surely beyond the human, beyond the subject-object structure. But that is just why revelation from "outside" is necessary. This is a basic idea implied by the incarnation of God. Therefore the revelation is God's own appearance within human space-time categories, within the subject-object structure. Consequently, humans are told who God is in ordinary, nontranscendental language. The incarnated God, Jesus Christ, can be described as a grammatical object. And the criterion for a correct apprehension of him are found within immanent, space-time reality. In ontological terms, the correlation between the divine and the human spheres of reality can only be understood correctly as the correlation between the incarnated's sphere of reality and the human sphere of reality. Self-transcendence is in the New Testament made superfluous.

God's transcendence is presupposed when the Bible talks about God revealing himself in history (cf. Rev. 21:6, Is. 44:6, Col. 1:17, Gen. 14:18, Ps. 57:3, 1 Tim. 6:15–16, John 1:4). Because he is transcendent, he has to reveal himself for man to know him. The living God is before, beyond, and independent of all he has made. He is before, beyond, and outside space, time, and all universes and everything that exists. Humans are not able to find and know this transcendent reality by their own efforts. But God's revelation, the Bible, carries the human mind beyond what an individual can teach him or herself. (Cf. 1 Cor. 2:9.)

This key concept of transcendence needs clarification.[6] It can be understood in two ways, each having decisive consequences. A limited negative transcendence is formally described as "A is not-P,"where only the predicate is negated. Thus, by saying what A is not, you indirectly know something about A. Absolute negative transcendence, however, is an absolute negativity, formalized as "A is-not P," where the link (copula) itself is negated. Christianity's concept of revelation is, according to its self-evaluation, best described as a revelation of absolute negative transcendence. This means that there is no possibility to say anything about God (or ultimate reality) in a limited negative way (for example, God is not a thing, not a person, or not an idea) or in a positive way (for example, God is depth, the absolute, or the creator), except when the special revelation is known and the assertions fit its content.

This means that Christianity cannot be subordinated to being a universal category of religion in which the different answers are but variations of humanity's search for ultimate reality, and of various cultures' efforts to understand and interpret our common human existence. Placed within these contexts, God's word would have to be understood as a revelation of limited negative transcendence, or possibly of positive immanence. Since reality after the historic fall is ambiguous, God would then have to enter a scene set by humans, reading a script made by humans. Theology would turn into anthropology.[7] When God's word and immanent reality are integrated in any of these ways, ultimate reality can easily be defined agnostically or atheistically (cf. Paul Tillich).

However, a revelation of absolute negative transcendence must (simply in order to be a revelation) be understandable to human beings living in this world's immanent reality. How then is this concept of revelation kept safe from ontologically being reinterpreted into a limited-immanent concept of transcendence? When revelation presupposes that absolute, negative transcendence appears in positive immanence (verbal language, the incarnation), this would certainly be possible. The horizon of the text would in such a case be subordinated to one's own immanent viewpoint or perspective.

This is avoided through two steps. First, one has to acknowledge the possibility that the connection between the Bible and absolute negative transcendence is real, and not reject it *a priori*. Second, one's understanding of the character and acts of God is exclusively bound up with the empirical environment within revelation itself. Criteria of analogous aspects to human experience in general are to be found only within the revelation. Biblical studies must keep this in mind in order not to change the object of investigation according to subjective presuppositions (cf. the question of the historicity of the miracles). The Bible is a book whose main body is characterized by concrete, realistic descriptions of distinct content. This would give the reader "a publicly accessible tradition of behaviour and language-uses" (cf. Wittgenstein II), especially by "the Old Testament accounts of God's saving acts in the life and traditions of Israel."[8]

What, then, is the common touching-point between transcendent and immanent reality, between God and humans, which will make revelation receivable by humans? The history of philosophy gives numerous examples of thinkers trying to develop a concept, an idea, or a category having such a universal character that it might be applied as a basic principle in understanding total reality. Theology likewise has searched for such a principle in order to make its speech about God possible, meaningful, and understandable.

The most comprehensive ontological principle used is being (cf. M. Heidegger, R. Bultmann and P. Tillich). Being is the most universal of all concepts, because being may be ascribed to everything, including God. Humanity is, the world is, and God is. Humanity has being, the world has being and God has being. This common touching-point may ontologically be defined in two different ways, corresponding to our two concepts of revelation. Either our understanding of being is based on a relative concept of transcendence, i. e., positive or limited negative being. Or it is based on a concept of absolute negative transcendence, i.e., a concept of being related to a revelation of God as absolute negative transcendence.

In the first case, being as universal principle is used as an integration point in which everything that exists participates. That does not necessarily mean there are no differences. The main thing, however, is that there is something which is in common in all of reality, something which transcends the separation of subject and object: being. This monism (or pantheism) applies to God and humans, nature and universe alike; there is no room for any part of reality to be excluded from being subordinated to being. Therefore a concept of transcendence can only be understood in a positive or limited negative way.

When a concept of God is connected to absolute negative transcendence, however, there can be no integration point between God and the universe or humans. Being as the point of contact is then understood as a universal link (copula). Being is here analytically without content; it is a word or a code which is used to tie certain explicit or implied predicates to a subject or an object. This is also the ordinary usage of the word to be, or being. Verbal language, according to the biblical ontological structure, is the point of contact between God and humans. Verbal language is ontologically capable of communicating absolute negative transcendence to the human mind, created in God's image. This does not imply that God and humans are integrated. What it does mean is that humans may correctly apprehend ultimate reality, God, communicated to us by the words of revelation.

God and humanity, then, are seen as a polarity. A polarity consists of two distinctly separated opposites which do not exclude each other, but are conceptually interdependent. There is in the Bible a polar structure between God and the universe, subject and object, good and evil, truth and falsity, light and darkness, (God's) holiness and love, salvation and perdition, etc. Concerning the latter there is a polarity within the concept of salvation itself, as the cross of Calvary signifies what happened with *God* only, because of humanity's moral rebellion against him. *Humanity,* then, is saved (placed in an eternal personal relationship with God) through faith in what *God* has done. Men and women are justified through something *outside* themselves, i. e., the work of Christ (cf. the polarity of faith and works).

This view implies an emphasis on the "propositional" nature of the Bible, communicating knowledge from God to humans. This does not exclude the sound hermeneutical principle of interpreting each text according to its individual literary form. What it does mean is that God is able to communicate with humans (created in his own image) in a way which gives humans precise, if not exhaustive knowledge about both transcendent and immanent reality. To define revelation exclusively as symbol and myth is to push the concept of God in the direction of "the wholly other," beyond precise description in subject-object language. But the Bible says God himself entered human reality as a distinct person in flesh and blood (John 1:18), describable in dynamic, concrete language.

The so-called "nonpropositional" view of revelation, however, is right in maintaining that the Bible is not *merely* a handbook of information and description, but that it also generates an existential "encounter" between God and humans. "At the level of experience, it is when a man so reads the text that he hears God, for example, *forgiving* him that the authority of the text is fully experienced." Nevertheless, "the point behind the so-called 'propositional' view is even more important," namely, "that the dynamic and concrete authority of the Bible rests, in turn, in the truth of certain affairs in God's revelation to the world. As J. L. Austin succintly puts it, for performative language to function effectively, 'certain statements have *to be true.*'"[9]

A Rational Examination of Biblical Truth-Claims

"Truth" is used in the Bible in several ways,[10] one being correspondence with the facts of the matter. How, then, do we decide whether biblical propositions correspond with the facts? This question has been thoroughly debated, especially since logical positivism argued that for a statement to be meaningful, it had to meet the requirements of empirical (instrumental) verification.[11] Later it was discovered that "the cognitive meaning of a statement in an empiricist language is reflected in the totality of its logical relationships to all other statements in that language and not to the observation sentence alone."[12] The foundation of a person's noetic structure can be seen as closely related to his or her whole way of living, his or her knowledge being subordinated to a given perspective, a paradigm.[13]

This does not, however, exclude the possibility of a rational examination of biblical truth-claims, integrated in the biblical worldview. But there is no room for proof in a strict logical sense. Logical rules will have to be applied in circumstances that cannot fully be described in advance. Thus there will always be an element of subjective valuation. Consequently one's arguments will take a *cumulative* form.[14]

One cannot say exactly when a paradigm, or worldview, will have to be abolished, but there might be a point where one's interpretations appear so strained that the assumptions on which they rest become discredited. For Christian apologetics it would in my opinion be wise to direct attention to the "humanishness" of humans,[15] the historicity of the resurrection,[16] and possibly also the universe and its form,[17] among other things. This would be done in order to show the correspondence between the assertions of the biblical perspective and objective reality. The latter is then presumed to give a witness of truth to the believer and unbeliever alike, since God created humans with cognitive categories that correspond with objective reality (outside the human mind). In practical life,[18] then, if not in theory, objective reality will function as a universal point of contact. This should make it easier for people of various backgrounds and beliefs to accept the content of the Christian revelation, as this is seen to fit the facts.

A Common Ontological Reference Point

Nevertheless, in order to make biblical ontology possible and meaningful in relation to other types of ontology, there is a need for a theoretical point of contact, an open concept of reality which would be able to encompass all ontological possibilities. This "meta-ontological" concept would have to reduce its own ontological content to a minimum in order not to exclude any other position. What then, is common to *all* ontological theories?

In asking what is real, we raise two questions. One is about the criterion of reality itself, the other is whether a certain object fulfills the criteria. Thus, we have one question about criteria, and one about (different degrees of) certainty. These two cannot be separated from each other. It is impossible to talk about an object (which does/does not fulfill the criterion of reality) without there also being a subject (which is certain/not certain whether the criterion is fulfilled). Reality, then, appears to us in both an objective and a subjective way. These two "modi" must be distinguished, but not separated.

An ontological concept acceptable to everybody cannot, however, decide which of these "modi" are the most important, whether anything objective exists, or whether we can know anything about it, etc. In these issues people profoundly disagree. Eliminating all matters of disagreement, the only criterion of reality left is a formal one, to be expressable in verbal language. The only "dogmatic" element here is the belief in language (widely understood) as the place where reality appears in both an objective and a subjective way. Ontological systems are dependent on the possibility of exact communication. Therefore language is the key to an "open" concept of reality. The concept of truth has thereby not been made relative. The only thing implied is that all possible positions are real insofar as they can be expressed in language. Reality is in this way looked upon as all-encompassing and ambiguous.

This includes the biblical concept of absolute negative transcendence, which in turn makes biblical ontology with its polar structure one among many possibly valid positions. One alternative, for example, are the Eastern and Heideggerian influenced positions, which seek to overcome the polar subject-object structure. In expressing their views, however, they are bound to use subject-object language. This fact does not exclude the possibility that ultimate reality transcends the distinction between subject and object. Likewise, those who would deny that language is a means of precise communication are bound to express their view through the same language.

My main point in this essay has been to specify the ontological structure which biblical language conveys. This in turn can be made communicable to other ontological positions through an all-encompassing "meta-ontological" concept. The reason for doing this is to secure the Christian faith from being perverted when placed within an ontological structure other than its own. Keeping the first commandment implies a clear knowledge of which concept of God is in question.

NOTES

1. Tillich's thought is supposedly well known. His main work is *Systematic Theology I–III* (Chicago: University of Chicago Press, 1967). As for reference works on Tillich, I am indebted to Aksel Valen-Sendstad: "Ontologiske implikasjoner i Paul Tillichs korrelasjonsmetode" (Ontological implications in Paul Tillich's method of correlation), in *Norsk Teologisk Tidsskrift* (Oslo: Universitetsforlaget, 1970), 30–61.

2. Man's sinfulness is understood ontologically, not as a personal, moral rebellion against the personal, infinite Creator.

3. Paul Edwards, quoted in John Warwick Montgomery, *Tillich's Philosophy of History*, in *Where is History Going? Essays in Support of the Historical Truth of the Christian Revelation* (Minneapolis: Bethany Fellowship, 1972), 135.

4. Cf. in particular Martin Heidegger and Zen-Buddhism. Another very interesting work which to a certain extent reminds me of Tillich is Robert I. Pirsig, *Zen and the Art of Motorcycle Maintenance* (London: Corgi Books, 1980).

5. Carl F. H. Henry, "The Interpretation of the Scriptures: Are We Doomed to Hermeneutical Nihilism?," *Review and Expositor* 71, no. 2 (1974): 206.

6. For this point I rely heavily upon Aksel Valen-Sendstad, *Filosofi til kristentroen* (Philosophy to the Christian faith) (Stavanger, Norway: Nomi forlag, 1973). See also his *Kristen dogmatikk* (Christian dogmatics) (Oslo: Luther forlag, 1979), pt. 1.

7. Cf. notably Immanuel Kant's transcendental idealism, where the object adjusts to the structure of man's mind. It is difficult to exaggerate how this perspective has influenced Protestant theology after Kant. A propositional revelation from God was ruled out *a priori* by Kant, and even if he had made room for it, it could not have given any knowledge about God, only about the religious capacities of man.

8. Anthony C. Thiselton, *The Two Horizons: New Testament Hermeneutics and Philosophical Description with Special Reference to Heidegger, Bultmann, Gadamer and Wittgenstein* (Exeter: Paternoster Press, 1980), 444.

9. Ibid., 437.

10. Cf. Ibid., 411–15.

11. Cf. Steven Holtzer, "Can We Talk About God? The Religious Language Controversy," *Trinity Journal* 6, no. 1 (1977): 57–72.

12. Carl G. Hampel, "Problems and Changes in the Empiricist Criterion of

Meaning," *Semantics and the Philosophy of Language,* ed. L. Linsky (Chicago: University of Illinois Press, 1952), 181.

13. I cannot go into the related debate between Karl Popper and Thomas Kuhn's positions on falsification and paradigmatic perspectives here; cf. I. Lakatos and A. Musgrave, eds., *Criticism and the Growth of Knowledge* (London: Cambridge University Press, 1970). My own view would be that of a "soft perspectivist"; cf. Louis P. Pojman, "Rationality and Religious Belief," *Religious Studies* 15, no. 2 (June 1979): 159–72.

14. Cf. Basil Mitchell, *The Justification of Religious Belief* (London: Macmillan, 1973).

15. Cf. Francis A. Schaeffer, *The God Who Is There* (London: Hodder & Stoughton, 1968), *He Is There and He Is Not Silent* (London: Hodder & Stoughton, 1972), *Escape From Reason* (London: Inter Varsity Fellowship, 1968).

16. Cf. Montgomery, pt. 2–3; Frank Morison, *Who Moved the Stone?* (London: Faber and Faber, 1930); Josh McDowell, *The Resurrection Factor* (San Bernardino: Here's Life Publishers, 1981).

17. Cf. A. E. Wilder-Smith, *God: To Be or Not To Be? A Critical Analysis of Monod's Scientific Materialism* (Neuheusen-Stuttgart: Telos-International, 1975) and *Man's Origin, Man's Destiny* (Neuheusen-Stuttgart: Telos-International, 1974).

18. Cf. esp. Francis Schaeffer's apologetics. As for the case for the historicity of the resurrection, Montgomery and others would claim a high degree of theoretical, empirical probability, independent of different "paradigms."

12

Talk of God and Minimal Judaism
ASA D. KASHER

Minimal Judaism

It seems difficult to offer interesting, correct generalizations about the Jewish religion. It seems impossible to put in a nutshell what bears the stamps of dozens of active generations, spread over so many different times and places. Any attempt would seemingly look hopeless to disentangle, within the sphere of Judaism, religion from surrounding cultures and from internal, national moods. However, all this is only apparently so. Appearance of diversity does not exclude an underlying essence. Under the title of "Minimal Judaism" I would like to point out the following essential ingredients of the Jewish religion.

First, Jewish religion is governed by *constitutive* rules. In other words, the religious code of practice should not be taken to play a major role within the religion, but rather be regarded as an implicit definition of the religion. Thus, whatever is part and parcel of the Jewish religion is shown in one way or another in its practical regulations, and in turn, in the overt conduct of not only the pious, but also in that of an ordinary observant follower of the religion.

Second, Jewish religion is *total*. That is to say, the ideal code of religious practice is complete, including regulations, whether general or particular, with respect to each and every sphere of given human activity. Most of the given domains of human activity are religiously neutral, the exception being what is deeply immersed in activities such as idol worshipping, which the religion resents. Given such a neutral sphere of human life, a typical religious problem takes the form of "How does one express religious values within that sphere?" The Jewish religion offers an abundance of solutions of such problems in areas such as work, food, family, etc. Practically every common area of private activity, from cradle to grave, is covered by the code of practice.

Third, the point of most religious regulations in Judaism is their being an embodiment of extreme opposition to any form of idolatry, in the broadest sense of the term. Since excessive devotion to anything in the world may render it being worshipped as what is of utmost importance, the Jewish antagonism with idolatry is not confined to classical idols, such as Baal, Zephyros, or Luna. Jewish religious practices are meant to express strong opposition to any form of addiction, be it to wealth or strength, love or lust, self or nation, or what have you. Roughly speaking, the Jewish code of religious practice consists of a variety of institutions of self-restraint, each directed against certain forms or dangers of idol worshipping or of absolute devotion to something worldly.

Thus, the three essential ingredients of the Jewish religion, according to the present point of view, are its constitutivity, totalism, and anti-idolism. These main claims of Minimal Judaism are, indeed, in much want of philosophical clarification and historical support, but since our present purpose is elucidation of talk of God in Minimal Judaism, rather than Minimal Judaism itself, we will leave it at that. For anyone who rejects the ideas of Minimal Judaism at the very outset, what follows may be considered as a philosophical exercise in understanding talk of God in a possible religion which bears some similarity to Judaism (or Islam) or some common brand.[1]

Talk of God: First Step

Talk of God seems to prevail in the history of Judaism. For Abraham, according to the Bible, God is "the Judge of all the earth" and it is unthinkable that he is "not going to do what is right" (Genesis 18:25). And then, for the author of Psalms, the Lord "is my shepherd, I shall lack nothing. In grassy pastures he makes me lie down; By well-watered resting places he conducts me" (Ps. 23:1–2). Saadya Gaon, who is considered to have initiated systematic theology in Judaism, wrote about God's incorporeity, arguing that the prophets saw just the created glory of God. Glory, in one sense or another, is also what several pietist Jews in Germany had in mind about three hundred years later—one of them writing a hymn of glory which reads: "His head replete with saving dew of light/ His curls still wet with dewdrops of the night," or "His head of plaited hair like that of youthful time/ His locks flow in black curls as they do in one's prime."[2] Could such a diversity of expression be dis-

168

tilled and made into a clear Jewish way of talk of God? While an ordinary view of Judaism seems to suggest an answer in the negative, Minimal Judaism holds a key to an affirmative answer.

The name of that key is, indeed, constitutivity. Not every phrase used by observant Jews with relation to their religion is strictly Jewish, committing everyone who attempts to draw an accurate picture of Judaism to include an explanatory logic or history of that phrase. Since, according to the view of Minimal Judaism, the Jewish religion is defined by a code of practice, just those expressions should be considered, when the religion itself is depicted, that play an official role in one of the institutions of the religion.

Now, there are two major texts which include ample talk of God and which have been granted a formal function by the Jewish religion, *viz.,* the Old Testament and the Prayer Book. We should, therefore, consider the nature of talk of God in these books in turn, in order to get an impression and then form a view of talk of God in Minimal Judaism.

Notice that by focusing our attention on these Scriptures we have not excluded the possibility of there being some form of talk of God used only by Jews in relation to their religion. However, even if there are some turns of speech which play a significant role, say, just in some Kabbalistic tradition of certain Jews, as long as these texts have not been canonized by the religion, within one of its institutions, they do not form a constitutive element of Judaism and do not represent the religion or part thereof in any way.

Holy Scriptures

Where does one make a start at characterizing talk of God in the Old Testament? Difficulties seem immense. Is it possible to bridge over differences between, say, talk of God in Job and Leviticus, or between God's strict justice, according to one chapter of Genesis, and his mercifulness, according to the next chapter, or, again, between a literal interpretation of Ecclesiastes and a figurative explanation of the Song of Solomon?

All these questions are far from being simple to answer. However, from the present point of view, many of these questions may, or actually should, be evaded. No reading of a verse, interpretation of a chapter, or analysis of a book may be ascribed to the religion itself, rather than to certain persons who observe it, unless they are reflected in the religious code of practice. What cannot be ascribed to the Jewish religion on the grounds of any of its rule-governed institutions should be consigned to an appropriate cultural sphere, but not to the religious core. Thus, whatever reasons might adduce for uses of talk of God in the Bible, the religious significance of these uses should be couched in terms of the religious function of the Holy Scriptures taken as a whole.

What is the religious function of those Scriptures? Generally speaking, such sacred writings are taken to provide foundations of one kind or another for the religion which sanctifies them. How, then, could a collection of chronicles, commandments, prophecies and the like underlie a code of practice?

To answer this question, let us consider, first, the way in which any traditional code of practice develops. When a new problem is encountered as to whether a certain action would be legitimate under some circumstances, a natural route is usually followed toward a solution of the given problem: very simple problems are decided by one's normative intuition; problems of higher complexity are litigated and then decided on the grounds of some explicit norms and implicit principles of various extents of generality; but every once in a while a brand-new problem appears, the solution of which requires new legislation rather than litigation or intuitive judgment. Legislation in turn may take the form of applying rather deep-seated, basic norms, but sometimes it requires recourse to the very foundations of the whole code of practice, in the last resort. This happens when the problem posed bears no significant similarity to any of the previously solved religious problems. The scarcity of such occasions does not preclude them from contributing in an important way to the development of the related code of practice, much beyond what meets the eye.

The need to reach the very normative roots of a code of practice, in order to solve a new problem which is encountered within its domain, is none too natural when the code of practice is that of a total religion. Clearly, a total religion is bound to face such problems, because it looks for appropriate expressions of its values in every human domain, utterly new ones not excluded.

Thus, sacred writings serve as normative roots of practice-oriented, total religions, such as the Jewish one, according to Minimal Judaism.[3] Notice that the Holy Scriptures are not required to lend an explicit expression of the underlying value of the religious code of practice. On the contrary, the common mixture of Scriptures of different literary forms renders the normative roots of the religion somewhat flexible, by being amenable to different interpretations. In a sense, Holy Scriptures provide the related religion with an outline of its limits, because whatever belongs to the religion must be either compatible with those Scriptures, under an appropriate interpretation, or else be incompatible with them in an internally justified way. Naturally, delimitation by chronicles, for instance, enables the religion to reach what is beyond any given collection of commandments or proverbs.

Talk of God in the Holy Scriptures should now be explained on that background.

Talk of God in Holy Scriptures

The most basic value enhanced by the Holy Scriptures of the Jewish religion, according to the present view, is against idolism. A hint at the basic attitude is to be found in the Ten Commandments, but in the second one, rather than the first: "You must not make for yourself a carved image or a form like anything that is in the heavens above or that is on the earth underneath or that is in the waters under the earth. You must not bow down to them nor to be induced to serve them" (Exod. 20:4–5). To be sure, the gist of this commandment is not the commonly understood condemnation of erecting religious statues and the like, but rather denunciation of every kind of active idol worshipping anything on earth or in heavens or waters. This observation is essential to the Jewish religion according to Minimal Judaism.

Talk of God in the Holy Scriptures serves mainly the purpose of underlying a code of practice which is meant to turn its followers away from every form of idolatry. Thus, talk of God does not here serve any assertorial purpose, be it theological, historical, scientific or what have you, but rather a normative purpose, directing the follower to observe an anti-idolist code of practice.

Let us consider a few examples:

1. The first verses of the Holy Scriptures teach us, I think, a clear lesson: What follows from saying ". . . God created the heavens and the earth" is simply that God is different from both the heavens and the earth, or in other words, that neither the heavens nor the earth should be worshipped.

The same interpretation holds for the whole story of the creation. It may be read as a suggestive catalogue of possible idols, each and every one of which "you must not bow down to . . . nor be induced to serve." Debarred from being considered deserving worship are thus the sun and the moon, and "the great sea monsters and every living soul that move about . . . and every winged flying creature" (Gen. 1:21), and last but not least, every human being, male and female alike.

2. The famous call "Let my people go" stands for personal and national freedom of the oppressed, but within the biblical contexts it carries quite a different message. That this is so is clearly shown by the literal context, i.e., the biblical verse which reads: "And afterwards Moses and Aaron went in and proceeded to say to Pharaoh: 'This is what Jehovah the God of Israel has said, "Let my people go that they may celebrate a festival to me in the wilderness,'" but Pharaoh said: 'Who is Jehovah, so that I should obey his voice . . .'" (Exod. 5:1–2). Thus, Moses and Aaron did not strive for freedom *per se*. The religious significance of national freedom is its possible, or sometimes necessary, contribution to religious freedom: Why should Pharaoh let my people go?—That they may celebrate a religious festival. Notice that the answer put into Pharaoh's mouth is also, first and foremost, religious: "Who is Jehovah . . .?" Many years later, religious abhorrence of nationalism would be nourished, perhaps more than ever.

3. The conclusion of the book of Ecclesiastes has been taken by many of its readers to be discordant from the teaching of the rest of it: How could "the conclusion of the matter" be that one has to "fear God and keep his commandments" (Eccles. 12:13), if "Everything is vanity!"? However, that discordance is only apparent. In the present religious context, vanity is not sheer nonsense. After all, "for everything there is an appointed time . . . a time to plant and a time to uproot what was planted; a time to kill and a time to heal . . ." (Eccles. 3:1,3). Consigned to vanity is everything which is not of supreme importance, but everything on earth is not of such an importance, because nothing should be idolized. Thus, in a sense, everything is vanity. That is what "fear of God," at the conclusion of the book, means: keep the commandments, which constitute a practical embodiment of the ideal according to which there are no idols that play their role in the life of humanity, or in biblical terms, the ideal according to which everything is vanity. How is the logic of talk of God in the Holy Scriptures thus interpreted? As a first approximation toward a full-fledged interpretation of talk of God in the Holy Scriptures, the following principles may be put forward: First, talk of God in the Holy Scriptures

is normative. What we mean by that is shown in the examples we have just considered. Every significant case of talk of God in the Holy Scriptures has normative consequences, and thus, as we all have learned from Hume, it has also a normative ingredient. The normative grain of that talk of God is expressed by taking the phrase "this-and-that is (a) God" to stand for "this-and-that may and ought to be worshipped." Distinctly, an idol is not (a) God, *ergo*, no idol may be worshipped.

Second, talk of God in the Holy Scriptures is exclusive. What is ascribed to God in the Holy Scriptures cannot, strictly speaking, be equally ascribed to anything in space and time. By talking of God, the Holy Scriptures should be taken to discredit the ascription of some property to anything in our world rather than credit with the same property some being elsewhere.

Hence, the exclusive reading of the biblical directive to "love Jehovah your God with all your heart and all your soul and all your vital force" (Deut. 6:5) is that ardent, complete, unconditional devotion to anything on earth should never be exercised. If what one loves with passion turns, say, into a moral monster, then if one's devotion remains intact, it means that the beloved is an idol, and whereas there is nothing wrong in the former, the latter is religiously resented by all means.

These principles form a rough, first approximation toward a theory of talk of God in the Holy Scriptures from the point of view of Minimal Judaism. A better approximation should provide a detailed analysis of the text, including reduction, interpretation or implication principles which are applicable to each and every verse of talk of God in the text, and should also provide a method of integrating talk of God in these texts with all the rest of them, where details appear of no obvious religious significance.

Prayer and Liturgy

Talk of God predominates also in the liturgical institution of prayer. Much of the Jewish prayerbook is adopted from the Holy Scriptures; most parts of the prayerbook are abundant in praise of God, e.g., "Blessed and praised, glorified and exalted, extolled and honored, magnified and lauded be the name of the Holy one, praised be He."

Presently, we would like to bring forward utterances that are made in profusion during a variety of standard prayers, *viz.,* requests that have the form of being addressed to God. Although such requests are not, strictly speaking, cases of talk *of* God, but rather cases of what looks like talk *to* God, they all carry presuppositions about talk of God, as we shall see in a minute.

Notice, first, the liturgical requests are apparently similar to ordinary ones. "Rebuild Jerusalem the holy city speedily in our days" is a request made by observant Jews after almost every meal, but a request of the very same wording could have been addressed to the mayor of the city or anybody else in an appropriate position. Now, a speech act of request is felicitous only if certain conditions obtain, such as the addressee's being assumed by the speaker to be able to do the requested act, or the addressee's not being taken by the speaker to be about to do that act anyway, and so on.[4]

Two of these conditions are of particular interest. When a real request is made the speaker believes that the addressee does not know that the speaker wants the addressee to do the requested act to an extent which justifies an overt approach. The speaker also believes that what he is doing is an attempt to get the addressee to do what otherwise he might have avoided doing. Hence, an ordinary request is made on the assumption of the speaker that a certain amount of ignorance may be ascribed to the addressee, as well as a frame of mind which is indeterminate in part.

Notice, second, that according to garden-variety theologies, common among Jews as well as among members of other denominations, supreme perfection implies omniscience and immutability. Thus, according to the popular, sung version of the creed "All-seeing, He knows well the secrets now concealed;/All outcomes from the first, to Him they are revealed" and according to Maimonides' *Guide of the Perplexed* the unity of God precludes God's mutability, since whatever can undergo any change is divisible.[5]

It should be clear by now that the latter theological claims are incompatible with the presuppositions made when liturgical requests are understood as ordinary requests addressed to God. This is a strict incompatibility between mutability and immutability, as well as between omniscience and ignorance in part.

Is there a way out of this liturgical, or rather liturgico-theological paradox?

Furthermore, a difficulty arises in understanding the concept of liturgical request, not only because a liturgical request takes the apparent form of a genuine request, but also from the liturgical nature of liturgical requests. How could a fixed formula of prayer reflect in a faithful manner the everlasting changes in the observant's frame of mind, beliefs, attitudes and feelings? Could a handful of fixed requests ever be useful under all circumstances, no matter who is praying, when, where and why? The obvious answer is in the negative, if liturgical requests are considered as real requests.

The solution we would like to propose is related to the phenomena of make-believe, shown by Frazer, in his *The Golden Bough*, to appear in various contexts of a formal nature. In some cultures, "a woman will take a boy whom she intends to adopt and push or pull him through her clothes; ever afterwards he is regarded as her very son, and inherits the whole property of his adoptive parents."[6] The Jewish feast of Tabernacles offers another example, where the observant Jew spends a week in what is formally regarded as a booth, as if he is wandering through the desert the way the tribes of Israel did after they had left Egypt. An as-if element plays a formal role in the Christian Eucharist, the Jewish poem addressed to the seventh day, during the service of the Sabbath, and the Passion Play of the Shi'a Muslims, where the sufferings and burial of Husain, son of 'Ali, are re-enacted.

What we would like to suggest is that every liturgical request in the Jewish religion is not a genuine request, but rather is on a par with requests uttered by actors during some significant plays. When an actor performs a speech act of request, it should look as similar to a sincere speech act of request as possible, though a hard core of insincerity cannot be removed, because the speech act is part of a play, of a formal as-if context. A liturgical request is uttered as if it is addressed to someone who is mutable, who does not know what the speaker is being exasperated by, a person who can be convinced to show mercy, exercise justice, or become passionate.

If prayer is a religious play, then no difficulty arises from its taking the form of genuine speech or from its having fixed formulas, since both of these traits are characteristic of speech acts within plays.

What is the point of such religious plays within Minimal Judaism? A person who beseeches someone else to be helpful, merciful or understanding has been entangled with some trouble that is out of control. But a person who admits being worrisome has also admitted having no grounds for any claim to the related supremacy, and what is less than perfectly supreme should not be worshipped.

Hence, human beings should not be worshipped if they are admittedly prone to weakness. The point of prayer, according to Minimal Judaism, is, then, the expression of resentment against any form of worshipping human beings, a point depicted in playing the role of naturally weak human beings.

In the present essay we have tried to show that various formal forms of talk of God in the Holy Scriptures and talk to God, so to speak, in the Jewish prayerbook can be interpreted, according to the principles of Minimal Judaism, as having mainly normative, anti-idolist implications. To be sure, what has been presented is a bare outline for a framework of interpretation. The elaboration of many details is a fascinating story for another occasion.

NOTES

1. I am here indebted to Y. Leibowitz, *Judaism, Jewish People, and State of Israel* (Tel-Aviv: n. p., 1975).

2. See Jacob J. Petuchowski, *Theology and Poetry: Studies in the Medieval Piyyut* (Cranbury, N. J.: Fairleigh Dickinson, 1978).

3. There is an important difference between normative roots and the so-called "basic norms." Whereas the latter take the form of a norm, the former do not have to.

4. For some additional conditions, see John R. Searle, *Speech Acts* (Cambridge: Cambridge University Press, 1969).

5. For an exposition, see Lenn E. Goodman, *Rambam: Readings in the Philosophy of Moses Maimonides* (Los Angeles: Gee Tee Bee, 1978).

6. James G. Frazer, *The Golden Bough,* abr. ed. (London: Macmillan, 1922).

CONTRIBUTORS

Samuel A. Adewale, Lecturer, Department of Religious Studies, University of Ibadan, Ibadan, Nigeria

John K. Ansah, Lecturer, Department of Religious Studies, University of Cape Coast, Cape Coast, Ghana, West Africa

Fritz Buri, Professor Emeritus, Basel University, Basel, Switzerland

A. Robert Caponigri, Late Professor of Philosophy, University of Notre Dame, Notre Dame, Indiana

Thor Steinar Grödal, *Cand. Philol.,* University of Bergen, Landas, Norway

Frederick M. Jelly, Prior, The Dominicans Priory of St. Albert the Great, University of Dallas, Department of Theology, Irving, Texas

Asa D. Kasher, Professor of Philosophy, Tel-Aviv University, Tel-Aviv, Israel

Eun-Bong Lee, Professor, Duk-Sung Women's College, Seoul, Republic of Korea

M. M. J. Marasinghe, Senior Lecturer in Buddhist Studies, University of Kelaniya, Minuwangoda, Sri Lanka

Mercy Amba Oduyoye, Lecturer, Department of Religious Studies, University of Ibadan, Ibadan, Nigeria

Samuel Rayan, Professor of Systematic Theology, Vidyajyoti Institute of Religious Studies, Delhi, India

Robert P. Scharlemann, Commonwealth Professor of Religious Studies, University of Virginia, Charlottesville, Virginia

INDEX

Index

Index

Ludwig, Emil, 70
Luna, 168
Luther, Martin, 145

Macquarrie, John, 54, 56, 57, 59
Magadhan Emperor Bimbisara, 111
Mahā Brahmā, 110–11, 115
Maimonides, Moses, *Guide to the Perplexed,* 174
make-believe, 175
Malebranche, Nicolas, 37
man-god, 45
Manoah, 8
mantras, 13
Mar Osthathios, Metropolitan, 151–52
Marduk, 7, 139
Martini, Simone, 45
Mascall, E., 60
masculine principal, 10–11
materialism, 106, 111, 158
Mbiti, J.S., 79
meaning, 139–41, 146–47, 157
mercy, 22, 58, 61, 64, 72, 82–83, 94, 175
Messiah, 48, 138
metaphors, 54–55, 92
metaphysics, x, 10, 41, 63, 88, 119, 125, 127–28, 151
Micah, 23–24
Michaelangelo Buonarroti, 46, 88
Middle Ages, ix, 17, 18, 59, 128
Middle East, 47
miracles, 101
Miranda, José, 9
Mirò, Joan, 37
missionaries, ix, 87, 111
monism, 139, 161
monotheism, ix-x, 153
Moore, Basil, *Black Theology a South African Voice,* 149
morality, ix, 63, 71, 101, 103, 106
Morris, Charles, 34, 39
Moses, 9, 16, 139, 172
Mother, the, 8, 10, 101
of God, 45
Murillo, Bartolomé Esteban, 88
Muslims: *see* Islam
mystery, viii, 12, 18, 24, 29, 55, 61, 89, 157
of being, 136, 139–42, 146–47
of God's name, 52, 54, 83, 104

mysticism, 6, 15–16, 17, 126, 129, 130, 142
mythology, xi, 4, 7, 54–55, 57, 89, 95, 139, 140, 146, 157

Nādānusamdhāna, 14
Nām Bhayan, 13, 14–15
Nāma Japa, 13, 14–15
Nāma Sādhana, 12–15
name-giving ceremony, 6–7
names, 15
definition, 116–17, 120–21, 124–26
etymology, 7–8, 68, 70–72, 74–76, 89–91, 92
of God, *see* Devine name
significance of, 5–7, 13, 67–68
Nārāyana, 13
Nāri, 10
nationalism, 168, 172
naturalism, vii, viii, 101, 105
nature, 20, 22–23, 98, 137–38, 161
God and, ix, 44, 87–88, 99–102, 105
Nazianzen, Gregory, 17
Neoplatonism, 116, 124, 125, 126, 129, 130, 153
new creation, 139, 150
New Ecumenical Research Association (New ERA), x
New Testament, 54, 158
Newman, John Henry, 33, 37, 48
Newton, Isaac, 37
nibbana, 111, 115
Nicaeno-Constantinopolitanum, 136
Nicene Creed, 56, 136, 150
Nicolas of Cusa, *De li Non Aliud,* x, 116–31
Nigeria, ix, 67, 79
nihilism, 141
nominalism, 4
nonbeing, 119, 124
nontheistic religion, vii, x, 106
Noth, Martin, 9
numinous, the, 29, 55
Nyame, 90–91
Nyankopon, 91

obedience, 10, 101
object, the, 61, 102, 116–17, 118, 124, 127, 128–29, 157–58, 159, 162

184

objectification, 140
Odomankoma, 90, 91
Old Testament, 6, 8–9, 54, 160, 164
Olodumare, 68, 71–72, 78, 79–80, 83
Olorun, 68–69, 70–71, 73–74, 78, 79,
    80–81, 83
Oluwa, 68, 70–71
Om, 11, 16, 20–23
omnipotence, 80–81, 89, 137
omnipresence, 82, 91, 93–94
omniscience, 81, 90, 92, 95, 174
onomatology, 117
ontology, xi, 60, 64, 142, 156–57, 161,
    163–65
Onyame, 90
Onyankpon, 90, 91
oppression, 8–9, 21–22, 23
Orient, the, 98–99, 105, 158, 164
Original Sin, 149
Orishas, 73
Otherness, 101, 116–31
Ott, Heinrich, 52
Otto, Rudolf, 29, 52, 53

Pali Canon, x, 107, 110–12, 113–14
Pannikar, R., 4, 15
pantheism, 151, 158, 161
paradise, 101
paradox, 95
parousia, 138
Pārvati, 10
Parrinder, Geoffrey, 85
Pascal, Blaise, 36
Passion, of Christ, 146
Paul, St., 40
Pentateuch, 9
Pentecost, 63
perception, 34, 61
perfection, 58–61, 115, 174
perichoresis, 143, 151
personal names, 124–26, 128
personality, 141, 160
    of God, 135–36, 146
personalism, 42
Petrarch, 46
Petrine, 46
Philo, *Life of Moses*, 16
philosophy, viii, 18, 87, 95, 98–99,
    120, 160
Plato, viii, 7, 41
poetry, 44, 46

polarity, 162
political activity, 99, 103, 150, 151
polytheism, 3, 151
poor, the, 22–23
post-mythical age, 54–55
post-structuralism, 38
power, 6, 7, 10, 119
    of God, 72, 75, 78–81, 87, 89, 92,
    104
Prabhu Jagadbandhu, 13
praise, 94
praise names, 91–93
prayer, 3, 17, 45, 47, 49, 73, 74, 76,
    101, 115, 173–76
Prayer Book, Jewish, 169, 173
pre-Aryan culture, 106
prejudice, 69–70
Preuss, Horst D., 9
primitive cultures, 44, 54, 79
problematics, 148, 149
Proclus, 120
progress, 36
prophets, 23, 103, 139
Protestant theology, 138, 157
proverbs, 76, 89, 93–94, 171
Providence, 94, 103
Psalms, 168
Pseudo-Dionysius, 116, 120, 128
punishment, 78–79, 81, 94
Purānas, 12–13
purification, 15, 17
Purusa, 10
Przywara, E., viii–ix

racism, 149
Rādhā, 10, 11, 14
Radhāswāmi Path, 14, 16
Radhakrishnan, 112
Rahner, Karl, 52
Rama, 14
Raphael, 45
rational-irrational, 136, 140–41
rationality, 136, 140
reality, 5, 7, 11, 18, 21, 22, 24, 29, 41,
    62–63, 127, 129, 130–31, 139, 140,
    159, 162–64
    different spheres of, 156–57, 160, 162
reason, 18–19, 60, 120, 121, 137, 138,
    140
rebellion, 21
rebirth, 111, 113

Stephen of Rome, 154
stoics, 3
Strauss, David Friedrich, 139
subject, 61, 102, 116, 128–29, 157–58, 162
subjectivity, 140, 158
suffering, 10, 88, 151
supernatural, 103, 115, 137, 139, 140
supranaturalism, ix-x, 100–1, 105
suprarational, 52, 58, 138
Supreme Being, 3, 63, 68, 69, 71, 72, 73–74, 76, 78, 79, 83–84, 86, 91, 97, 98, 157, 175:
  see also God
Suttas, Buddhist, 108, 109, 111, 112
symbolic language, 40, 43, 53, 56, 62–64, 102, 142, 152, 158
symbols, viii, ix, 33, 34–38, 40–42, 50, 54–55, 57, 136, 138, 140, 145
  religious, 54, 55–57, 62, 64, 89, 95–96, 103, 143, 146, 152, 157
synthesis, 127–28, 157

Talbot, Percy A., 73, 76–77
talking drums, 94–95
teleology, 140–41
Ten Commandments, 171
Tennyson, Alfred, Lord, 46
Tevijja Sutta, 108, 112
Thakkur Bhaktivinode, 13
theism, vii, 104, 106
theology, vii, 95, 102, 104–5, 116, 119
  Christian, ix-x, 17–18, 42, 105, 117, 127, 138, 148, 150, 157
  contemporary, 148–53
  dialectical, 116
  language of, 52–53, 62
  ontological, 156, 160–61
theon, viii, 38, 39–41, 50
Theotokos, 45
Thomism, 58, 60
Thyāgarāja, 14
Tiamat, 139
Tillich, Paul, x, 54, 102–3, 116, 156–58, 160
time, 37
Tolstoy, Leo, 46
Tower of Babel, 63
tradition, 6, 102, 148
trances, 113–14

transcendence, 33, 38, 40–44, 101, 105 141–44, 156
  of God, 15, 22, 19–30, 48–50, 82, 95, 102, 151, 159–60
  negative, 159–60, 161, 164
  properties of, 58
transfiguration, 47, 48–50, 54
tree deities, 111
Trinity, 146: *see also* Holy Trinity
Trikaya, 146
Trimurti, 146
Trinidad, 135
trope, 39–40
truth, 3, 5, 11, 35, 50, 58, 64, 120, 121, 140, 141, 150, 162–63

Ugga, 111
ultimate reality, vii, ix, 7, 52–53, 57–59, 61, 88, 96, 106–7, 156, 159–60, 161
Unā Haimavatī, 19
unamable, the, 12, 15–20
Unamuno, Miguel, 34
unconscious, 46
uniqueness, 79, 149
unity, 3, 4, 10, 49, 114, 127, 131, 135, 149, 150, 151, 152, 153, 174
Upanishads, x, 12, 16, 17, 19–20, 108, 112

Varnātmaka, 13
Varuna, 3
Vāsettha, 108–9
Vatican, 153
Vedas, 3, 13, 18, 108
Vedic tradition, 107, 112
Vessavana, 111
Vijayakrsna Goswamin, 13
Virgin Mary, 45, 47
Vishnu, 7
Visnusahasranāma, 7
von Rad, Gerhard, 8

wars, 89, 100
Western society, 31, 32, 35, 37, 70, 102
Whitehead, Alfred North, 35
will, of God, 98, 142

Index